The
Smoky Mountain
Cage Bird Society

The Smoky Mountain Cage Bird Society

AND OTHER MAGICAL TALES
FROM EVERYDAY LIFE

JOHN SKOYLES

KODANSHA INTERNATIONAL
New York • Tokyo • London

Kodansha America, Inc.

114 Fifth Avenue, New York, New York 10011, U.S.A.

Kodansha International Ltd.

17-14 Otowa 1-chome, Bunkyo-ku, Tokyo 112, Japan

Published in 1997 by Kodansha America, Inc.

Library of Congress Cataloging-in-Publication Data

Skoyles, John.

The Smoky Mountain Cage Bird Society and other magical tales from everyday life/John Skoyles.

p.   cm.

ISBN 1-56836-181-5 (hc: alk. paper)

1. Life.   I. Title.

BD431.S584   1997

814'.54—dc21   97-2762

BOOK DESIGN BY LAURA HAMMOND HOUGH

Manufactured in the United States of America on acid-free paper

97 98 99 00   *Q/FF*   10 9 8 7 6 5 4 3 2 1

For Olga and Gerry

Contents

Acknowledgments

MY THANKS to Sheree Bykofsky for her encouragement and support and to Janet Rosen for her intuition. I am grateful to my editor, Nancy Cooperman, for her vision in shaping this book.

The

Smoky Mountain
Cage Bird Society

Harry's Card

I'VE TAPED on my wall a big index card that embarrasses me. I keep it here because I want to be reminded of my stupidity and maybe learn something from it.

One day I had a terrible time with my six-year-old son. He was fighting in first grade and we had to pick him up at the principal's office where he was rude. He threw things around his room, wouldn't eat his dinner, and when it was time for bed we were sick of each other.

Propped up against pillows, I read to him, as I do every night. When I finished the story and I was as tired as I had hoped him to be, he said, still full of fury, "I'm running away from home."

In exhaustion, I blurted out, "Send me a card."

My son suddenly sat up in bed, misunderstanding me completely, thank god.

He said, "Okay, Dad, you write a card to me for tomorrow morning and I'll write one to you." He had perceived my exasperated remark as asking for an exchange, and he beamed over it.

"Okay," I said, and he hugged me hard for the first time all day and we kissed goodnight.

At the dining room table, I made a card for him, using his crayons, with a drawing of flowers in a vase. The next morning he drew one for me and brought it into the kitchen.

It's that large index card on my wall. It says at the top, "To John," with a backward "J" and then there's a box filled with many colors. Underneath, it says, "Love, Sun."

The poet William Wordsworth wrote in another century, "The Child is Father to the Man," and my son's suggestion was one the father should have made. He didn't need to keep my drawing: the sign of our exchange was enough for him. But I do need to post his card in front of me: it's a colorful commandment to love.

Good Luck Charms

ON THE NIGHT I left New York for Dallas and my first real job at age twenty-two, my father walked across the living room of his three-room apartment in Queens, took the ring from his pinkie finger, and gave it to me.

He said it was for good luck. It had been his father's stickpin, which my mother had made into a ring for him, and now he wanted me to have it.

I had seen it on my father's hand all my life, but I had never really looked at it. A thick gold setting surrounded a deep orange stone, a carnelian. On the stone was a delicate engraving of a woman in a long robe; at her feet, a little boy carried a tray. I was touched. It was a memento of the living, an inheritance without a death. I thought this was the best way to give something, not in grief but in gladness and with hope.

Since then I've become a collector of such talismans, and an instigator of many such gifts among my friends.

When my friend Jean was having a rough time, I received in my change at the post office a quarter painted entirely green—and it was St. Patrick's Day! I mailed it off to her immediately. Years later she returned the odd favor: a quarter glossed bright red, which she received in change on St. Valentine's Day. It was the perfect switch, and I have her quarter today.

A lot of people carry good luck charms. The poet Frank O'Hara wrote:

Now when I walk around at lunchtime
I have only two charms in my pocket
An old Roman coin Mike Kanemitsu gave me
and a bolt-head that broke off a packing case
when I was in Madrid

They remind you of those you want to be with and provide a kind of company as you walk around or sit at your desk. In a way, they're portable friends.

My grandmother used to say that if you looked in a boy's pocket at the end of the day you would always find three things: a piece of string, a button, and some seeds. This is from the old country, and today I know it would be different, with a Nintendo cartridge probably being part of the inventory. The point is that children know enough to carry their own charms, and the old are wise enough to observe them.

When you give someone a charm, you risk being scoffed at, but it's a chance worth taking. Most everyone values a silly object, and the sillier the better, because it's more memorable.

I have on my desk a cigar box containing an assortment of these talismans. There's a piece of Carborundum steel, for sharpening knives, that's about three inches long; a friend gave it to me on a trip we took. I like the frayed and ancient leather that houses it, too. There's a crushed Gauloise package, a beautiful blue that doesn't look like a commercial product but like something that fell from a collage. My uncle smoked Gauloises, filling the air around him with their pungent aroma. I have a few clay pipestems that washed up on the beach here and are from another century. My friend, a sculptor, gave them to me. I have a pen made out of wood, a gift for serving as a best man to my best friend. Sadly, the marriage ended before the pen ran out of ink, but talismans can be of that kind too.

The ring is my favorite. Notice that the rings of fathers appear on the hands of their sons—usually too late for the fathers to have the pleasure of giving, and too late for their sons to say thanks.

I'm glad my father let me wear his stone before either of us lay underneath one of the large drab ones that will mark our places.

Midnight the Cat

I'M NOT WILD about cats, but when we moved South, my wife promised our six-year-old daughter a kitten, and I went along with it.

When I was a kid, our neighbor was a grouch who growled at any cat that passed his door: "What good is he? He can't give milk like a cow. He doesn't love you like a dog. You can't ride him like a horse. He's just a pest, no more than a pretty rodent!"

We made fun of old Mr. Borst, but I never could shake his words from my mind, even though I knew they were the opinions of a crank. When our cat knocked a glass of water onto my newspaper, I'd ask myself silently, "What good is he?"

My daughter named him Midnight, because he was totally black. My wife picked him up one afternoon at a public swimming pool. The lifeguard's cat had a litter, and the kittens frisked around the pool all summer, and people took them one by one. Midnight's fur was worn away on his back haunches from scampering around the rough concrete. He looked as if he was wearing one of those sport jackets with patch pockets on the elbows.

My daughter taught him to fetch or rather he very naturally fetched the paper balls she threw, bringing them back and dropping them at her feet. When she dressed him in daisy chains, he never seemed to mind. One day after a visit to a friend's house, she started calling him by the strange name of "Missy Foos." Her friend's family was from Chile, and they told her that Missy Foos was the most popular name for a cat in Chile, in the same way Rover used to be in our country for a dog. When I met the friend's mother, I asked her what was the most popular name for a dog in Chile. Her response: George Washington! And so we had a Missy Foos, and the crazy name seemed to fit.

When the cat was two, it got sick. I remember the afternoon my wife and I stood in the veterinarian's office and got the diagnosis: megaesophagus, meaning an enlarged esophagus. The vet read the definition to us from a huge textbook and told us the cat couldn't keep food down and would have to be destroyed.

Seeing how distraught we were, he said there's one thing we could try for a few days, and if it got him through, he might be home free. I agreed to try anything, because I didn't want my daughter to come home from school to find her cat gone forever, without even a good-bye. Still, when we told her of his condition later that day, she used the past tense even as the cat whisked past her feet, and she cried, "And he was such a good kitty!"

I knew it was worth trying what the vet had prescribed.

Following his directions, my wife put cat food, a can of liver-flavored paste, into the blender with a glass of milk and made a puree. She filled a turkey baster with the stuff, and my job was, as the vet put it, "to hold the cat vertically" as she fed him.

I knelt on the floor, holding Missy Foos upright. At the first touch of the turkey baster to his lips, he tossed his head, splashing my face, hair, and neck with the rich, fragrant mixture. My wife laughed and that made me laugh too as we finally did the job.

It had to be done three times a day, and each time I dressed in an old yellow slicker and wore a polka-dotted shower cap. I was like a worker in a car wash, but what splashed me was worse than sudsy water. We got through the weekend and went back to the vet.

After examining Missy Foos, he scratched his head and said, "He seems okay. Maybe it wasn't megaesophagus," and he returned to the heavy book, whose thin pages made an awful sound as they turned. "It was probably esophagitis, which they can get over."

Needless to say, we did not return to that vet, but Missy Foos flourished, although he developed a case of asthma as time went on and made a breathing sound like the last bit of water going down a drain. So it was asthma shots every six months, and now he's twelve years old.

And I've found a use for him after all. In the winter, he lies in front of the wood stove. He lies far away when the stove is really burning, and when it needs wood, he lies close to it. He's like a furry barometer, gauging for me when I have to add wood to the stove. He's good for that at least, if I want to feel practical about it. And if I don't, he's proof of something else: what we do out of love for each other. If it wasn't for him, I wouldn't have had the chance to don a yellow slicker and shower cap, and kneel on the linoleum floor holding an animal vertically. And my daughter would never have seen her father making this awkward prayer out of love for her.

A Brother's Love

I USED TO TAKE my Chevy to Joe's Mobil for gas and service. My father told me, when he gave me my first car, a 1962 Mercury Comet, to get gas at the same place all the time. Then take your car there when it needs servicing, so they know you and value you as a customer. It was good advice.

Joe is a short, stout fellow with horn-rimmed glasses. His office is always crowded with old ladies reading the newspapers and drinking coffee, which they make in a big metal pot. They are not his customers but his sisters and their friends. Joe is an easy-going guy and lets them hang out there in the mornings.

Joe runs the place with the help of his brother, Ralphie. Ralphie is tall, slow, and gangly. His job is to pump gas. He doesn't work on the cars; the most he does is rotate tires outside the main office. Ralphie doesn't say much, only the same, "Yup, yup," to whatever you say to him, whether it's "Good morning" or "Nice day." When there are no cars to fill up, Ralphie just leans against the pumps, watching the traffic go by, wholly engrossed. Every so often, one of the ladies comes out and brings Ralphie a cup of coffee and a doughnut and he nods and continues staring.

One day when I took my car in, I saw that Joe had hired two boys in their twenties to help him with the repair jobs. A radio played rock music from the bays and there was shouting and laughing where before there had only been Joe tapping around an engine with his tools.

"Business must be growing," I said to Joe as he took my keys.

"I'm thinking of getting out," he said.

When I came back to pick up my car, there was a gathering around one of the bay windows. A car had been rammed through the garage door, breaking the glass and buckling the metal. Ralphie had been driving. The two boys couldn't contain their laughter, and Joe was talking to Ralphie, whose head hung down into his dark blue shirt.

I decided to wait in the office, and then I noticed Joe following me in, with his arm around Ralphie's waist. The boys were still laughing.

Joe's face was filled with pain for his brother and anger toward the boys. I could see he didn't know what to say to them: they were possibly going to buy him out and he didn't want to alienate them.

In the office, Ralphie got his cotton jacket, zipped it up, and walked home.

Joe gave me my keys and I paid him.

When I opened the door to my car, I heard him yell at the two boys, "There was a reason that happened. It was not Ralphie's fault. That car is lacking a master cylinder." Then his voice dropped, and he continued, "However, it could have been avoided."

Joe had to defend his brother, yet maintain his integrity

as a mechanic, and he did it well, as paradoxical a task as it was. The boys stopped grinning. As I drove off, Joe was bringing out big sheets of plywood from the rear of the garage to cover the empty place where the window had been.

Joe did sell out a few months later, and after one visit to the new boys I never went back. They were not good mechanics, as cocky as they acted. They did a tune-up on my car and left one of the spark plugs hanging out. I brought it back after I got about eight miles to the gallon and the engine rocked and bounced when it ran.

After that, I saw Joe around town occasionally, always followed by Ralphie. One time they came out of a florist, Joe carrying a large planter containing a three-foot palm tree. Ralphie trailed after him, begging, "Can I carry it, Joe? Can I carry it?" Very gently, Joe turned and placed the urn into Ralphie's hands. It was as if he were handing him a globe, a small version of the world, fragile and precious. It was a risk Joe had taken all his life; when Ralphie's face widened into a great smile, Joe lost his exasperated look, smiled back, and they walked down the avenue together.

There was only love between these two brothers, despite all the heartache each of them must have gone through in their lives together. Life would have been easier if Joe had not given his brother a job, easier if Ralphie had not tried to drive during those last months, but then it would have been a life of avoidance, a life of no commitment.

Joe could have lived a life in which accidents "could have been avoided," to use his own unforgettable words, and yet he chose a richer, harder life, one based on love.

Seeing

DID YOU ever notice how people see what they want to see? They will overlook dramatic flaws in their finances and when confronted with them, will make extravagant excuses. Or when buying a house. Once they've fallen in love with a place, they won't give up on it, despite reports from the exterminator, despite warnings from the building inspector. Everything seems cosmetic compared to the fundamental love they feel for the house, which they see as overcoming all problems.

Funnier still is how used-car buyers invent stories regarding the goodness of the previous owners.

"I think he was a Chrysler executive who lived alone and just drove long distances on weekends and took great care of it. Only the driver's seat has a spot of wear on it."

Or:

"He must have been a soldier stationed in Germany, and the army shipped the car back here for him when he got transferred. So he bought it cheap over there and that's why the price is so low now."

They see what they want to see.

———

WHEN I WAS A KID we moved to a neighborhood in the suburbs. My father was disappointed because there was no local bar. He liked the company of neighbors in a neutral place. A few weeks after we moved, he came home overjoyed. I heard him telling my mother about a bar he passed, right next to an inn, a mile or two from our house.

"I saw a man playing pool there," he said.

"Not true," she said.

"He was, honey, and all the bottles were lined up behind him," he insisted.

My mother said it was impossible and, to avoid an argument, my father asked my mother to meet him there the next night when he got off work. If he was right, she would have to buy him a drink. If she was right, he'd take everyone out to dinner.

My mother met my father at the place, the same time as the night before. She arrived there just as the barber began to sweep his floor with a longhandled push broom, which my father had mistaken for a pool cue. Behind him were the rows of bottles of hairdressing preparations and tonics that my father had transformed into Jack Daniel's and Dewar's.

He had seen what he wanted to see, and now he would pay.

We all went to the Villa Bianca for spaghetti, and my father sat surrounded by his family, who teased him for his wild imagination and praised my mother for seeing what she wanted to see and making it happen: a dinner out.

Yet

THE RINGING in my ears did not stop for weeks, so I went to the doctor. Test upon test indicated that I might have a tumor, a brain tumor, a growth on one of the seven nerves leading from the brain.

I would have to have an MRI to determine the tumor's size and whether it was cancerous.

The problem was that there was no room available on the MRI machine. I would have to wait a week.

It was a funny week. Everything that bothered me before, all the tasks that disturbed me, I found I loved. When my son woke up in the middle of the night, I realized I liked rocking him back to sleep. I treasured the interruptions, because they meant *I was still around to be interrupted.* I learned to accept the interruptions for what they were: just as much a part of life as what was planned.

At work, I did not become alarmed at small crises and disasters. I was able to keep them in perspective and calm those around me as well. What I wanted to say to those who worried over a printer messing up a job or our being late for a deadline was, "You don't know what a small thing you are worrying about."

I was getting sentimental, and I gave myself the freedom to feel that way. When you think you might not have long to live, you treasure even making a left turn out of your driveway. Every dog's bark becomes something to appreciate.

My wife went with me for the MRI. When I emerged from the lab, a neurologist showed us the film. "There is a small tumor, but from its placement and size, this is almost always benign."

We stopped at a bar on the way home and had two Jack Daniel's before we told anyone the news.

I was shocked to hear myself leave this message on the answering machine of my best friend, the first person I called: "The MRI showed the tumor is benign, so I'm not going to die." Stunned by that last phrase and the power that death had held over me in the last week, I added, with a laugh, the truth of all our lives—"yet!"

Country Living

WHEN WE LEFT THE CITY and rented a big drafty house on a lake, we had a lot of adjustments to make. First, there was wood. We heated with a woodstove, and I had never even had a fireplace. I found I enjoyed chopping the logs, seeing the way they split and smelled, and how they stacked up. You quickly appreciate the product of your efforts, unlike office work and other jobs I've had, where the satisfaction comes later. Chopping wood is simple: it splits and stacks right before your eyes.

The first time I stacked wood, I got carried away. I laid it wide and high. Our house stood at the top of an incline, a brambly, leaf-strewn hill, thick with trees. An elderly couple lived down the way and across the street. They sat on their porch in the afternoons, after they worked their little farm, he in overalls and a straw hat; she in a housedress.

They sat on that porch the afternoon I called my wife to help me stack what I'd split. The two of us took great delight in the job. I could tell my wife was impressed with the result of my few hours' work: enough to keep us warm for a week. We stacked it and stacked it. It was symmetrical and fragrant and we kept stacking. Our row was at least twelve feet long

and then we made it tall. When we had stacked it as high as
our heads, I noticed a slight tremble to the row, then a wobble.
I did not stop but stood on my toes, reaching higher, overreach-
ing, and then it happened. The pile, now over six feet high,
bent toward the incline and slid down in the most gentle and
graceful way. I should have been horrified, but I was too
stunned. I recall no sound from the toppling wood, only its
descent in a flood of triangular and lovely shards, a tide of oak
making its way back to the woods.

But I do recall another sound, it was a long peal of laughter from the little cabin across the street and, as my wife and
I looked over, we saw the old couple gazing up and howling
at us so that we too began to roar. It would be a long day,
bringing that wood back up by the armful, but a lesson had
been learned, privately and publicly, and it leveled the height
and distance between me and my neighbors.

The second lesson involved animals. In the city we rarely
even had mosquito bites. I guess the air was too poor for them
and they moved on. At this house, there were rabbits, chip-
munks, and moles. Our cat chased the moles and when he
caught one, it made the worst tiny screeching sound and we
all moaned in sympathy.

This house had a deck off the kitchen, the first deck we
had, and we loved to sit under the big oak tree next to it and
have iced tea. Our son, Harry, was a toddler then and our
daughter, Kate, was seven. She sang and drew pictures, and he
waddled around putting acorns and everything else into his
mouth. One evening the cat brought a mole to the party, just
dropped it at our feet, with feline pride. The poor mole was

still alive and the first to see it was my son, who, when I glanced over, was bending above it. Delighted, he extended his pointed finger. The terrified mole stood on its hind legs and promptly bit Harry's finger, drawing blood. My wife whisked him away, the cat pounced back on the mole, and my daughter dropped her crayons. I wanted the mole for rabies tests and had to compete with the cat for it. The cat picked the mole up in his teeth and ducked under the table and through the chair legs. He hid under the old grill and dropped the mole but quickly seized him back.

My wife was yelling from the kitchen, "Be sure to get the mole! Don't let him get away!"

Finally, I trapped the cat under my daughter's legs and he dropped the mole. This presented another dilemma: I did not want to be bitten, but I didn't have gloves, so I scooped the mole up, and flung him into the nearest container. In this case, it was the salad spinner my wife had been using on the picnic table. The poor thing gasped his last there, among the iceberg and chicory, and I placed the lid on him to make sure he wasn't faking.

My son was fine, but the vet suggested that I take the mole to the state lab the next day and have it tested. He said, "Just to make sure, even though there hasn't been a case of rabies around here for a hundred years."

I put the dead mole into a Ziploc bag and then into a brown paper bag before placing it into the refrigerator as the vet suggested.

The next morning, I grabbed it and took it to the lab before work.

The woman at the desk was very pleasant, and I found myself shy as I explained what I wanted. I brought the bag out of my attaché case and handed it to her. I glanced away, shyer still, as she removed it. Then I heard her say, "What's this?"

Above her paperwork, she held out half of a peanut butter and jelly sandwich! I had taken my daughter's snack! And that meant my daughter would yank a mole out of her lunch bag in front of all the other girls! I asked if I could use the phone and called my wife.

Hearing me on the phone, the woman at the desk said, "Make sure she puts it back in the refrigerator."

"Make sure you put it back in the refrigerator," I said. Then my wife went to the school to get the mole back, which she did in time.

The mole did not have rabies, my daughter did not have an unusual scare, my wife forgave my mistake, and I forgave her for getting upset on the phone. We forgave the cat for being the cat, but whether the mole forgave the cat is a question for those smarter than me.

My Road to College

I WAS THE FIRST PERSON in my family to go to college. When I was in high school, I had no idea how to apply to college and no one in my family knew anything about it either.

My father bought me a copy of *Esquire* magazine, the back-to-college issue, and it frightened me. Picture a kid in a lower class section of New York City turning page after color page of photographs of men leaning their gleaming wingtips on the bumpers of red sports cars. And guys in soft cashmere standing around the patio of a mansion with martinis in their hands. I was sure college was not for me.

But a funny thing happened, something totally unrelated to college: my Uncle Fred died. At his wake, I met a few relatives and friends of the family who asked what I'd be doing when I graduated from high school, and each recommended a college. The funeral director's son went to a small college in Massachusetts. A friend of my uncle's recommended an Ivy League college, and an aunt praised Fairfield University in Connecticut.

I was glad to know what to do, and I applied to all three.

I was not accepted by the Ivy League college but was by the other two.

I decided on Fairfield, but I almost didn't make it to the first day of orientation because of a dead dog.

My Uncle Pete was given the job of driving me, and he helped me pack my stuff in the trunk. We drove away from my neighborhood honking the horn, with my mother crying and my father waving from the sidewalk in front of our railroad flat.

All was going well until we got on the Grand Central Expressway by Shea Stadium. It was a horrible stretch, full of big holes and heaves in the road. The lanes were strewn with mufflers, fragments of crates, exhaust pipes, and other mechanical gizmos. Abandoned cars lined the side of the highway like the fossils of dinosaurs.

My uncle was telling me about a Bob Hope and Bing Crosby movie he had seen. They both played college students and wore raccoon coats. I was looking over at him and laughing when his eyes grew wide at what he saw ahead of him in the road. As I faced forward, I saw in the middle of our lane the carcass of a dead dog, a big German shepherd. My uncle looked left and right, but because of the heavy traffic, he had no chance to swerve. He hit it dead-on, and the impact made a sickening scraping sound that continued because we were now dragging the dog. Pete could not shake it loose no matter how hard he steered the car into fishtails. He pulled over and, when we got out, we saw the stiff legs of the dog caught up into the exhaust system, as if trying to lift us off the ground. The eyes of the dog were still open and it looked more like a statue than a once living thing. Worse, it looked like it meant to stay there. We could not pry its paws out from under the car where they were lodged.

"This boy's been dead a long time," my uncle said.

When the tow truck came, it hoisted us high and then the driver yanked the dog down, cursing as he held it by the sides of its chest.

I was afraid of being late for orientation, but my uncle calmed me down.

"A year from now, you'd be throwing that dog in the trunk, to put into the dean's office, or something like that." True prediction.

For the rest of the ride, we watched with delight as the landscape shifted from the worn tires piled on the edges of the city's muck to the wild swans in the lakes of Westport and Southport.

We made it on time and, while I was at college, I thought how the road out of the place you grew up has many detours, and I never forgot how I got there, hearing of colleges from those at my uncle's wake. And how I almost didn't get there, impaled by the legs of a German shepherd with rigor mortis.

Two deaths. One showing, the other hindering, the way.

A Story
My Mother Told Me

WE ALL LOVE STORIES OF SUCCESS, especially when triumph follows failure. Success after undeserved failure is the grandest, because there's a sense of justice in the world and a bit of revenge on fate.

In fact, success following failure is twice as sweet as success from the start. It's like sliding into a warm bath after being cold. It feels better than if you were warm in the first place. Athletes try harder against the team that had no use for them; stories fill the business pages about those fired from a company who later make a tremendous comeback and buy their old place.

My mother told me a story when I was a kid, and I've never forgotten it.

It was about a janitor at St. Mary's Church in New York, the church she went to as a child. The janitor's name was Fred Morgan. He did his job well, raised a family, and liked his work. She said he would sometimes give the kids the candles that were broken and bent, unworthy of the altar, which they would take home to their mothers.

Then came a new monsignor, who made all the teachers

take tests, reshuffled the priests to different duties, and had interviews with all the church staffers.

Although things were running along fine, he wanted to raise the standards of the church, so he issued new dress codes for staff and rules and regulations for the clergy. Among the new rules was one that all employees of the church had to know how to read and write.

This seemed a simple thing, except to Fred, who hadn't learned, and he was forced to leave his job.

With the help of a few friends, Fred set up a little tobacco stand, renting a corner in the back of a Woolworth's. He did very well and soon paid off his backers. He opened another stand in another Woolworth's, and that too did well. He did this several more times and, as the years went on, he became wealthy, sold the chain and retired early.

My mother said she saw him on a local news program, as he had become well known, not only for his success, but for his story. He still could not read or write.

She said that the reporter had admired how he had arranged his franchises, selected the spots, hired the right people, and so on. At the end of the interview, the reporter sighed and said, "Mr. Morgan, you have done so well these last years in the tobacco business. Just think where you might have been if you had learned to read and write."

After a pause, Mr. Morgan looked at her and said, "I know very well where I'd be. I'd be the janitor at St. Mary's Church on East Twenty-second Street."

Aunt Linda

MY AUNT LINDA never married but lived with her mother her whole life. We are Italian, and my grandmother was a great cook. She made everything from scratch, and it was not unusual to see her bed covered with a clean white sheet, and resting on top of it, large circles of flattened dough sprinkled with flour, to be used for ravioli. It was a cozy apartment, made cozier by the fresh flowers, good food, and the canary that sang constantly.

Linda worked for the purchasing agent at Paramount Pictures, ordering drapes for the executive dining room, inspecting linen invitations to first nights, and catering screenings and openings.

Each night I took the elevator up to Linda's office from the mailroom where I worked and we left together for the subway. Crowds on the train made conversation impossible, but on the walk home, Linda gave me her opinions of the top executives: Turner from Harvard, very tough; Blomberg, very shrewd; Colombo, a gentleman. She wanted me to emulate them, to be captivated by her descriptions, to be serious and suave. She'd say, "Colombo comes in from upstate, where he has a mansion and two mastiffs. You know what they are? Big dogs that guard estates in England. He told me." When she spoke like this, she smiled a smile that pictured me on such an estate, on my way up from the mailroom, all the way to the top, into the company of these men, protected by mastiffs.

But I hardly saw them. I dealt with those outside their doors and, in this way, I learned volumes from the porters, air conditioning men, and elevator operators.

Every two weeks, on pay day, Linda took me to lunch, to places she thought a man should know, where a boy should learn to be comfortable. There were German restaurants filled with heavily carved furniture; sporting spots with paintings of hunting dogs on the walls, and suits of armor in corners; delicatessens where the sandwiches were named after the city's sports heroes; steak houses where mats of beef hung over the edge of the plates and a potato cost five dollars; sections called "men's grills," where women were not permitted unescorted, and on entering one of these, it hit me: Linda was showing me the world but showing it to herself as well. She would never, and in some cases, could never, have gone to these places alone.

To teach me to pay a check, she slipped me folded bills under the tables of the Blue Ribbon, Luchow's, the Pen and Pencil, Sardi's, and Jack Dempsey's. All summer I pretended to pay and she pretended to be treated by her escort.

I did see the city in this way, and in her old-fashioned, well-intentioned chaperoning me around, I learned to see what I might never have. Linda handled herself beautifully in these public places, although perhaps in many cases they were as new to her as to me, though she never let on.

I had no role models of urbanity in my neighborhood except for one, and it was a woman, a woman who lived with her mother among the flowerboxes and pasta dishes of Queens, and who treated her nephew like a man so that he'd become one.

La Panza's Coffee Shop

I HAVE NEVER described the following incident to anyone. It was one of those whirlwind experiences that you know happened, but later seems like a dream, foolish to retell. But it is something that has always stayed with me, because it was the only time in my life so many angles intersected my path at once.

It happened the summer I was offered a teaching job at a college in Westchester county, just outside of New York City. I was out of work and happy to have the position. But the campus lies in a quarter mile of the most prime real estate in the country, and my teacher's salary could rent nothing nearby. Buying was entirely out of the question.

We had to find a place by fall, when classes started, and so my wife and I left our six-year-old daughter with friends and looked around. We had a big task ahead of us: moving, finding a place to live, a school for my daughter, and a job for my wife. Driving around in an old Chevy, with all the money you possess in your wallet, and visiting high-priced real estate offices is not the most heartening way to spend a summer.

Westchester was out. We walked through the beautiful towns where the streets were lined with bakeries and toy stores selling bright objects made of wood and not the plastic, mass-produced stuff. We bought our daughter a ballerina an inch high who danced in front of a mirror, motivated by magnets. We stopped for a danish at a pristine bakery. Clearly, we would have liked to stay there, but just as clearly, we were visitors. There was nothing to rent in our price range anywhere nearby.

We started moving north, up Route 95, through Connecticut, the towns of New Canaan, Greenwich, Green's Farms, and Darien. In Darien, when we walked into a real estate office, an agent came over and said, "Renting, right?" Was it so clear that we were not prepared to buy anything, and did it have to be said so publicly? Yes to the first question and no to the second. We learned the hard way that these places were not for us.

Finally we came to Bridgeport. I had lived there years before, having gone to college nearby. The dormitory I was supposed to live in hadn't been finished on time, and the contractor had to put up all the students at the Holiday Inn in Bridgeport. After two days, we were forbidden to call room service—but that is another story.

Still, I knew it was an interesting town, and I had gone to the P. T. Barnum museum with my friends. I can still picture Tom Thumb's bed, a tiny construction covered by a patchwork quilt.

In downtown Bridgeport, my wife and I bought *The Bridgeport Post* to check the classifieds, and went into La Panza's coffee shop. It was not like the coffee shops of Bronxville, which are bright and shining. La Panza's needed to be painted, its windows washed, its floors refinished, but it had an inviting warmth. A little neon sign surrounded by a circle in the front window read, SPAGHETT. I looked carefully: the "i" had not been burned out, but was intentionally omitted, an Italian dialect.

A group of men drank espresso and laughed and joked at one of the tables.

As we drank our coffee at the counter and paged through the paper, the owner watched us. Soon he came up and asked what we were doing. We told him.

"Hey, Joe," he called over to the table.

Joe came over and, after talking with us a few minutes, said that his father-in-law had a place to rent, right down the street. He sat next to me, and as we warmed to each other, he said he could even get the rent lowered, and the price he quoted was already something we could afford.

The owner poured us more coffee and we were excited.

When Joe found out my wife would need a job, he yelled over to Gerry who joined us. He was the shop steward for the local UPS office and he said he'd help out.

"The hours might be funny at first," he said, "but they'll improve as you're there." He gave us his card.

Meanwhile, Joe made a call from a phone behind the counter and I heard him making a deal for us on the apartment. He was saying, "Nice people, quiet, take a little more off." He put down the receiver and wrote a number for us to call.

The owner put hot muffins in front of us.

"My treat," he said.

My wife told the owner about our daughter and asked what the Bridgeport schools were like. He called to another man at the table.

Bill took a stool and his cup was refilled. He said he worked for the school system and knew every school in the area. He said that the one near us, where my daughter would be going, was terrific. A few of the others were not so hot.

We couldn't believe it. We were lining up an apartment, a job, and a school, all in an hour at La Panza's.

When they found out we had to move, they called to another man. He had just started a moving company and he too gave us his card. Our heads were spinning and they spun faster as we drank cup after cup of the strong coffee.

Soon, all of the men left their table and sat at the counter, surrounding us and talking about our plight.

"Your father-in-law's place needs paint," one yelled to Joe. "I'll do it on the weekend."

"The school will be good for the little girl," I overheard Bill say to some of the men, as he turned on his stool, his back against the counter. "When I clean the restrooms there, they are always immaculate, not like the other dumps nearby where they wreck everything."

I guess that judging a school by the condition of its bathrooms might not be the worst gauge, but it was not exactly what we thought of first.

Other men gave us their cards, warmly, and vowing discounts. One sold furniture, another worked for a gas station, a third installed lines for the cable company.

"Forget cable," another man said, sipping his coffee. "I'll

give you a little black box that gets everything and it's free."

The owner's wife brought out a tray of pastries and everyone helped themselves, complimenting the chef. The cash register hardly rang. It was more a clubhouse than a business, and after a week of being shown the door at real estate offices, we felt welcome.

We left there buzzing from the caffeine and the company. Our heads were spinning as we looked down the empty street, at the bright yellow light of the cafe window.

Back in our motel, we spread the cards and phone numbers out on the bed. It still seemed unreal: Nice Italian Boy with Truck Movers; Phil's Service Station; Jilly's Auto Glass; and the restaurant itself, La Panza's Coffee Shop and Bakery.

But we did not call any of the numbers. We did not believe them. We followed Groucho Marx's principle that he did not want to be a member of any club that would have him. We were used to being excluded, and this inclusion stunned us. Besides, the men, the shop, the coffee, all seemed unreal. We felt we had to suffer to get these breaks.

We continued up the coast to Rhode Island and settled in Providence. I commuted for three years, right past Bridgeport. Six months into my job, I got off Route 95 and tried to find La Panza's, with no luck. I still had the card, but when I found the address, there was no sign of its ever having been there. A warehouse stood in its place and when I went into a barbershop farther down the street and showed them the card, the barber said, "That place has been closed for years. For years."

I got back in the car and went home. It was one of those things that you think ceased to exist because you did not take advantage of it. I wondered if we too would have disappeared if we lived down the street in the father-in-law's place. More probably, we would have been found, by the little pocket in the city, by the warmth of strangers. I felt that our doubting its existence made it vanish. But a little of it remains, here in these paragraphs and every place where strangers open themselves to those in need, even if the need is not a desperate need, but one that can be met by a simple cup of coffee, some talk, and a push in the right direction.

The Feast of Fools

ONCE I HAD an opening in my office for a clerical position, a job requiring simple typing and filing. One of the applicants, a twenty-year-old named Fred, worked in another part of the company, but when he saw the announcement on the bulletin board across from the cafeteria, he called for an interview.

When Fred showed up, he took me by surprise: he was over six feet tall, muscular, and wore his blond hair in a braided ponytail that reached past his waist. He also sported a pinkie ring in the shape of a skull. He was a pleasant fellow and I wanted to give him the job. Then I checked his references.

A former boss said he had come to work drunk several times. Another said he dealt drugs. His current supervisor mentioned that he did the work but had missed a lot of days and seemed lackadaisical.

Still, I couldn't reconcile the warm person I met earlier with these references, so I called Fred back for a second interview. Even though this was a minor position, it was important to me because I had only two other workers in my small department. I asked him about any problems he might have had.

He admitted to some difficulties in the past but said they were over. I believed him and gave him the job.

Fred turned out to be terrific. He was tremendously conscientious and courteous. On top of that, he was tremendously strong and could lift heavy stuff with ease. Several months later, when I met his old boss, he asked me for the secret that made Fred such a wonder.

When my assistant left, I gave Fred that job, and he excelled there too. In his place I hired Anna, a quiet girl who wrote poetry. A few weeks later Fred called me at home one morning. He was laughing and said, "There's a surprise for you in the office, and it concerns Anna." He wouldn't tell me what it was, so I rushed in.

Anna looked up shyly when I approached her desk. She was wearing a kerchief around her head, but even with it on, I could see the surprise: she had shaved her head.

"It looks good," I said, and went back to my office.

Now I had three workers: an older woman, a man with a braid, and a bald girl. My department was getting a reputation for weirdness and the other supervisors kidded me constantly.

But I enjoyed it. We were a productive team, and now we had flair as well. When we sat together in the cafeteria, heads turned constantly. Over time, Fred and I became friends. He told me how he had been waiting for the chance to prove himself. Through his current job, his self-worth had been given back to him.

I don't criticize my colleagues in this company, but I have noticed that some of the supervisors were too supervisory, too superior. To keep my perspective on my position, I had a day each year in which I did the job of the newest person in my office and they did my job. I got this idea from an Elizabethan tradition called "The Feast of Fools," in which for one day everyone in the town reversed jobs. The mayor did the stable-boy's job, and vice versa.

It was a literal rendering of the old saying, "Put yourself in my shoes," and we all got the chance to look through each other's eyes.

And isn't this what art is: looking through someone else's eyes? When you see a painting, you view the world as the artist saw it. When you read a letter, a newspaper, or a novel, you grow in sympathy for others. Through these things you understand a little better what it's like to turn the key to the door of your neighbor's house, and walk in.

Generous Strangers

AS A KID, I spent a lot of time with my friends at a very small and rundown amusement park named Adventurer's Inn. It was one of those places on such a tiny budget that one attendant ran two rides. As soon as he loaded customers onto the Tilt-a-Whirl and sent them flying, he'd dash over to the Ferris wheel, help passengers aboard, and pull the lever.

On one night, we had spent our allowances in the shabby arcade, trying to win at Skee-Ball so that we'd get some coupons to redeem for prizes, prizes like plastic Hawaiian leis, tiny combs, rubber mice, glow-in-the-dark rings. As I was looking into the glass case, trying to make a choice, I felt a tap on my shoulder. It was a hip teenage guy with his arm around a girl. His hair was greased back (this was the fifties) and he wore a loud shirt. The girl had a ponytail; that's all I can remember about her. But there is a snapshot in my mind: the two of them looking over at me, both smiling, as they watch my reaction to the fat stack of coupons the guy has placed before me. The stack is multicolored. It contains coupons of the greatest value which I have never seen before. It entitles me to pick from the highest shelf: binoculars, a radio, a stuffed lion.

I have forgotten what prizes I chose, but I still recall the gift pile of coupons.

It was a small thing, but I've never forgotten it. And I've always wondered why they did it. Had they looked around and seen that this worthless junk was only a bother? Were they late for a movie? And why me of all the kids filling that place? But I was not asking questions then, I was beaming in a puzzled yet totally happy way.

There's a kind of giving to strangers that has grown legendary: Elvis Presley giving a car to a girl driving a clunker who compliments his Cadillac when they meet at a gas pump. Sam Walton, the founder of Wal-Mart, is said to have written a check to a waitress for $10,000 because she went across the street to get him a potato as there weren't any on the menu. Those are the dreams of the masses taking flight, to make up for the way things usually are.

But among most of us, those who ride buses and stand in lines, getting something from a stranger is memorable. When a bus gets stuck in traffic for a long period of time, watch how people pass their newspapers around. When a plane is snowed in and a flight canceled, people chat and joke with the children of those couples who are having a tough time keeping their kids amused.

Once I was on line in a supermarket with my Aunt Linda. We stood behind two small boys who were buying ice cream bars. Just as their turn came, they dropped their change to the floor, where it rolled under the counter and among everyone's feet. When they retrieved their coins, they were missing a quarter. The cashier had a patient but worried look as they searched along the floor and the line grew longer. Suddenly my aunt bent over, reached down, and said, "Here it is!" and she held up the quarter, which they handed to the cashier. I was pleased that my aunt found their money, but I was more pleased that she had first opened her purse and taken that quarter out without anyone seeing her.

I remember best an encounter with an elderly lady who I sat next to on a plane. She read a book that kept intriguing me, and I kept stealing glances at it. Finally I asked what it was: W. H. Auden's *A Certain World: A Commonplace Book*. It's his collection of the interesting quotes he wrote down over his lifetime, including some thoughts of his own. The woman asked if I'd like to take a look at it but I declined, not wanting to disturb her any more than I already had.

I changed planes and she continued on, but as I eased into the aisle, she handed me the book.

"It's a double," she said, "I have two of them."

When I hesitated, she said, "I love it so much that I buy one whenever I find it in a used bookstore. See?" The name of a library was on the inside of the book, and it was stamped DISCARD by the library for who knows what reason.

After a little back and forth, I accepted her gift.

On the next leg of my trip, I paged through it. Quote after quote engaged me:

"What friends really mean to each other can be demonstrated better by the exchange of a magic ring or a horn than by psychology."

"A man is infinitely more complicated than his thoughts."

"If the rich could hire other people to die for them, the poor would make a wonderful living."

I was tired from the trip. I kept putting the book into my jacket pocket and then, curious, taking it back out, to read another line or two.

I looked to it as someone looks to a sidekick or traveling companion, for a comment on what's happening in front of them, or maybe just because nothing is happening. It made instant company for that day, and its pleasure has lasted more than twenty years.

My feelings for that old woman are similar to those I have about certain teachers or coaches from my childhood: I wish I could have thanked them more. At the time, I didn't realize how much their gestures would mean to me.

Her example has given me a funny kind of courage, to give something to the person who isn't expecting it: a book I love, the tape I'm listening to, even knowing that the gift might be met with the greatest suspicion.

But when we part, they'll have with them an amusing companion, a pocket keepsake.

Somewhere I read that we take into the next world only those things we have given away here on earth. If that's true, my generous stranger will have her book with her and more.

A Memorable Christmas

I HAVE ALWAYS FOUND Christmas a bittersweet holiday. I think it's because it has such a long and cheerful buildup that when it arrives there's always a bit of a letdown. And the day itself begins to fall apart with the kids, when dinner is just about to be served, and they've already broken a toy or two, and they're hungry from frolicking among a houseful of wonderful odors with nothing to eat. At this point they begin to stamp and cry and they run to their mothers. But sometimes something happens to save the day.

I'm sure everyone has a memorable Christmas they can point to. Mine took place when we held it at our house and invited all my relatives and some friends in the neighborhood who had no place to go.

Our small town on the ocean was in a real and serious emotional depression. A fishing boat had been lost at sea two weeks earlier, and the fishermen's bodies were found one by one. In a tiny village, the loss of men whom everyone knows puts the whole population into a depression. Photos of memorial services covered the paper, as did tributes to each of the men. Each day another body washed ashore, until only one was missing, and that man's family was denied his life insurance payoff because his body had not been found and there was no written record that he had been on the boat. The insurance company insisted they needed proof of his death and would not accept the word of his family. It was a mean-spirited performance by the insurance company, and Christmas seemed out of place in such an atmosphere. Neighbors waved to each other with a defeated flipperlike gesture, more like a half-hearted karate chop than a greeting.

The week before Christmas, my son was a wreck, asking, "Can Santa see your thoughts?" and fearing his mind would be read and his secrets judged. In his life, Santa had replaced God for these weeks. So when the big day arrived, he was more upset and excited than he would be usually.

We had invited an older Portuguese woman who lived alone in the house next to us, and she announced at dinner that she had bought everyone "underpants" as gifts and she hoped we liked them. At her request, I had earlier carried in several boxes from her place, and I couldn't imagine underwear being in them. We had heard that she might be getting senile, so as the presents were unwrapped, there was more than the usual nervousness—until her first box was opened and my wife pulled out a beautiful new omelet pan which we had all heard, through her thick accent, as "underpants"! There was great relief as well as pleasure at the gift.

My son received what he wanted: a remote-control car. It was hard to get him out of the driveway, where he had the little racecar zipping this way and that, trying out its speeds. At one point he ran in yelling and, when the family and guests rushed to the porch, we found ourselves staring at what had disturbed him. Up in the sky a huge eagle circled the little truck from Radio Shack, thinking it was a new kind of prey! I took the controls and the eagle followed as I ran the truck to the end of the driveway and back. Then I scooped it up, thinking he might carry off the present, which would have left my son crying and the eagle in a field somewhere with a beak full of gears. It was a magnificent bird, and its appearance gave the feeling of a blessing.

At the end of the day, a neighbor phoned. It turned out that the lost fisherman's body still had not been found, but his jacket had washed ashore, and in that jacket was a key, and that key fit the door to his house, and with that key was the proof of who he was and that he was on the boat. The family's lawyer said that would be proof enough; he was sure the insurance company would accept it. The fisherman's family would be taken care of as well as could be expected under the circumstances, and the cloud lifted from our house and eventually from the town, even in this tragic aftermath.

So Christmas was a decent day after all, full of understanding and misunderstandings, natural surprises, expectations hopefully fulfilled, the defeat of a heartless bureaucracy, and a union around a table that left us with the feeling we belonged somewhere.

Raccoons

I HAD READ about raccoons, seen them on TV and in magazines, but I never really lived with them until we moved into a rural area.

In the middle of the night, my wife heard a noise and woke me. I sat up and listened: it sounded like someone dropping tree stumps onto the porch. I raced down the stairs, flicked on the porch light. A fat raccoon faced me, having knocked over a thirty-gallon garbage can, spilled and shredded the contents over the deck, and chewed a great part of them. He looked up blithely, holding the bone of a chicken leg in his paws, and went back to eating. When I slid the glass door open and started out, he waddled slowly away, looking back at me, annoyed by my lack of generosity. We heard him back again an hour later, but there was nothing we could do, so we let him feast.

The next day, I went to the hardware store and bought bungee cords, the kind wrapped in colored cloth and used to strap packages onto bicycles. We looped these over the tops of the trash cans, hooking them to the handles. That night, I heard the toppling cans once more, and when I ran down, there was the raccoon, delving in. The cord was next to the can, like a ribbon that had been removed from a Christmas present. The raccoon was muzzling a pile of rice—how wonderful that was to clean up from the rough deck the next morning.

My wife kept mentioning a shed, a small slant of wood that would hold two cans and that came with a heavy lid that slams down. To avoid that expense, I bought extra-heavy black bungee cords, so thick and wide my wife could not put them on or remove them, and I strained as I stretched them over the lids.

That night, more tumbling. This time I smiled, knowing the cords could not be removed. Downstairs, I saw they held the cover on tight, but the can was on its side, and somehow the raccoon had stuck his paw in and dragged out some baked beans.

A line from an old grade school book popped back into my head, buried there for almost forty years: the raccoon is capable of opening clams with his paws. This was cause for respect, but respect was not what I felt as I called the carpenter about building the shed for our trash cans.

We took to storing the cans in the basement until the carpenter arrived.

When I came home from work one night, I saw something strange in my backyard. It was not a shed, it was not a little place for storing cans. It was a tiny house. My wife met me in the driveway, very pleased. The little house cost only a bit more than a shed, and we could store the lawn mower and my son's bicycle there as well.

Now I had to thank the raccoons not only for many mornings of greasy cleanup but for a new debt.

A week later, I took a business trip to Texas, to the city of Austin, a beautiful place with mountains and lakes. On one of my free nights, I drove around the hills and pulled over to a roadhouse that looked friendly enough: a sign in front advertised Lone Star beer and one in the window promised live entertainment.

It was just after seven o'clock, still early for a roadhouse to get lively, but I was glad to gather my thoughts while sitting at the bar. The bartender was friendly and so were two other guys playing checkers. A big maroon curtain hung behind the bartender, as if a stage was hidden there. Another sign on those drapes announced: LIVE ENTERTAINMENT 8:00.

As eight o'clock neared, I asked the bartender who was going to perform.

"Just wait," he said.

At five to eight, I asked again.

"You'll see soon enough," he said. One of the other guys said, "You won't be disappointed," and whistled.

As I was wondering just what kind of place I was sitting in, the bartender left his post and walked around to the kitchen. He went out the backdoor carrying a garbage can, which I thought nothing of at the time.

At eight on the dot, he returned and filled my glass, tapping his knuckles on the counter, signaling my drink was on the house. I thought he might be trying to bolster my courage and that I was about to see the wildest floor show ever seen by a city slicker in this remote part of the Texas countryside.

Then with a big flourish, the bartender yanked the sash on the drapes and they jumped back.

What I thought would be a stage was a window and what I thought would be wild, was wild. Wilder than I could have imagined. And it was also "live," as advertised. The window looked out on the bar's backyard, some big boulders and bushes, and around them were the scattered chicken bones and ribs from the roadhouse's garbage, freshly scattered there by the bartender.

Little by little the "live entertainment" appeared: several big raccoons ambled over the rocks and began to gnaw and chew the bones. My eyes must have widened and my mouth dropped, because the men laughed, and laughed hard, pointing at me. Then I began to laugh too, all the more because of the feeling that the pests followed me right to Texas.

Charlie Hays

I ONCE WORKED for an organization where there were a lot of writers around, but the best storyteller of them all was not a writer. His name was Charlie Hays and he worked as the janitor of the place.

Charlie did the maintenance for a high school in New Jersey all his life and retired to Cape Cod. His wife died of cancer shortly afterward, and Charlie went broke paying her medical bills. He needed another job, so he came to work for us. He's probably around eighty today and still working.

Charlie was stocky and had a huge stomach, but it looked good on him, as it does on baseball managers. He had a face that hung above his chest like a cloud, but there was always a little curl at the edge of his mouth, just waiting to expand into a smile. When you saw him walking toward a leaky roof, you couldn't help picturing him in a baseball uniform, a coach strolling toward the mound, hunched over, ready to take the ball from a tiring pitcher and set things right.

From his first day, Charlie leveled all pretensions. Our organization gave grants to artists and writers, and was well known in the world of "the fine arts." Whenever Charlie

needed help from a repairman of one kind or another, he phoned from my office, and the whole place shook as he identified
himself: "This is Charlie, over at the Fine Arts."

Then he turned to our staff to explain what was happening. His gravelly voice made it sound like we were a gym, a
club, a powerhouse of physicality. He'd say, "Roderick's men
are coming for the cesspool," or "Ronnie Silva's boys are re-
wiring the barn." There was always a manliness about the way
he described them, as if they were an outfit in the army, coming
to attack.

Charlie was at his best when he passed through the office
just as someone mentioned a subject that interested him.

He'd stop dead, hammer at his side.

"Drunk?" he'd ask. "Did I ever tell you about the time a
still exploded on a farm in Teaneck and all the animals drank
from the stream?" He ticked off the species with his fingers,
"drunken cows, drunken horses, the sheep were drunk, every
one of them sliding around the pasture. It was Gambo's farm,
an Italian guy, but not with the mob. No. Called him Gambo,
because he had one leg." And with this he clasped his open
hand around his thigh to show where the leg ended.

At one point, I began to notice a peculiar thing about
Charlie's stories. All of the names of the people in them had
something to do with their jobs or their physical characteristics.
Gambo, for instance, means leg in Italian. He's told me about
a chef named Quattropane, meaning "four loaves of bread." He
knew an albino girl named Neva for snow and a bookie named
Furlong.

Once he told me about his friend Sam Quish. Sam is about the same age as Charlie, and he paints for the fun of it, big abstract paintings. When Sam signs his paintings, he uses his first initial and last name: S.Quish. It looks like "Squish," and some critics have used the word to describe the way the paint thickens on his canvas. According to Charlie, Sam had his eye on a widow, Mrs. Reed.

Charlie said, "For years he told me he wished he could put his social security check together with hers. So last month they got married, and he got his wish. But now he has another wish too; now he wishes he was never born."

I loved Charlie's amusement, too, at some of the plights he was called on to resolve. I told him once that a resident had a leaking stove.

He looked at me.

"That's what she said, Charlie, a leaking stove."

When he returned, he had a fake annoyed smile on his face.

"I fixed her leaking stove," he said.

Then he told me.

"When I get there, she shows me the water all over the floor, right under the stove. Before I check behind to see what's what, I pick up a rusty kettle on the burner. It had a hole in it, so when she filled it up, to make tea or something, the water came down."

All the young writers sat around when Charlie talked, and I could tell that not only did they admire the tale, they were memorizing details. But this is okay. T. S. Eliot said, "Good writers steal. Bad writers imitate." Charlie would have to pull himself away to get back to work because they kept pumping him for more.

There was another side of Charlie, the one that baked cakes, pies, and Irish soda bread and brought them to potluck dinners. I can see him now at the door of an office Christmas party, bending over to show two children his loaf of bread and explaining what it is. The children leave with a piece and he says to their mother, "The price of currants is outrageous, I tell you!"

Many have stolen stories from Charlie, as I've just done. And we could also do well to steal some of his character, his persistence in the joys of life despite its losses, and his continued patching of the holes in things.

Other People's Mail

MY NIECE and her friend were visiting, and one night I stumbled into a conversation the two teenagers were having about sin. In a corner of my living room, each described sins they had committed and felt bad about.

My niece said she was sitting in the subway one night, next to a man who had had too much to drink and who fell asleep. She said he kept nodding onto her shoulder and she kept gently pushing him back. In one of these pushes, his fedora fell off and landed on the floor. They were sitting right near the door to the next car, which was open. She said the hat kept moving closer to the open door, and she wanted to grab it, but was afraid. Suppose he woke up to find his hat in her hand? And if he stayed asleep, should she try to place it back on his head? As she was debating this dilemma, the hat blew right out the door, out the coupled cars, and onto the tracks. She said she still worried about it and thought her reluctance to take a risk was a sin.

My niece's friend then recounted how she had opened her boyfriend's mail once and found he was seeing someone else when she was gone for the summer. She regretted this "sin" as well. Noticing I was listening, they looked up at me and asked, "Have you ever read anyone's mail?"

I thought about it. Yes, I had. I told them the story. I was living on the second floor of a three story house in Providence, Rhode Island. I had become friendly with the fellow upstairs, Nathan, a quiet guy who had replaced two very noisy, very big men, whom the landlord nicknamed "The Clydesdales" because of the way they pounded and shook the house when they walked up and down the stairs. I was delighted with Nathan's quiet ways and hoped he would stay for a while.

One day he told me he had applied for a better job with Wang, the company he worked for, but the position was in the Boston office, an hour away. He had just graduated from college and had been with the company for only a few months, but he thought he would try for the promotion. It would mean a pay raise and he was excited about that, but it would also mean moving. I encouraged him, but in my heart I selfishly didn't want him to leave.

The three apartments all received their mail through the one mail slot in the downstairs door. Each tenant picked out his own and left the rest on the stairs. One afternoon, while sorting the mail, I saw a letter to Nathan from Wang's Boston office. There's the answer, I thought, and as I put the envelope on the stairs, I noticed that it was not sealed. It had been stamped by a postage-metering machine which had somehow missed sealing the envelope. I was dying to know if Nathan got the job. There was the open envelope before me. I reached in quickly, all the while glancing out the front door in case one of the other tenants, including Nathan, was coming, and I pulled out the letter. I read the first words, "We regret" and, knowing then that Nathan didn't get the job, I quickly folded the letter back into the envelope, this time licking it and sealing it.

Then I saw something that shook me, made me nervous in a way that comes only when you have done something stupid or wrong and get the feeling that someone has seen you. I saw, as I returned the letter to the pile of Nathan's other mail, that it had been sent in a window envelope and that I had neglected to fold it back in the same way it arrived. The result was that where Nathan's address should have appeared, there was in its place a white space, a plain blank surface that glared through the window. Obviously the letter could not have been delivered that way. There was only one thing that could have happened to this envelope: someone opened it, read it, and sealed it back! And I was that person.

I took it and ran up the stairs to my apartment. I paced around the kitchen table where the envelope shone in the sunlight. Then I remembered a technique for opening mail I read somewhere: I rolled a pencil under the flap and it came open. I folded it properly, resealed it, and ran back to the vestibule.

My niece and her friend were laughing, but the thought of this episode had me nervous all over again.

"That was the first and last time I've read anyone's mail," I told them, hoping to sound wise and experienced.

As I turned from them, I overheard the friend say, "Even though it was funny, it was still a sin."

Exquisite Sensitivity

MY SON HAS A FRIEND, Jake, who is a sweet little boy, but he has a problem. He is very sentimental and tender, too frail for the world of second graders, in which he often rises to a challenge only to get bruised, a defeat which he dwells on at length and in detail.

Because of a divorce, he has only one parent, who must work long hours, so I volunteered to take Jake to Boston for some tests that the school requested. One of the doctors was a friend of mine, and taking a trip to the city with this boy was something I was happy to do.

Jake talked a lot on our two-hour drive, about dinosaurs and basketball among other things, and then he fell asleep. One of the striking things he said was that he doesn't like his mother to wave to him after she drops him off at school. "It makes me feel sad to look back at her," he said. It is that kind of tenderness, which sometimes led him to depression, that the school wanted evaluated.

I enjoyed chatting with my old psychologist friend, and then he took Jake for two hours of testing. Afterward, Jake and I had lunch, because he had more testing with a neurologist and a psychiatrist later in the day.

In Cambridge, I decided to buy Jake a treat to help him through his ordeal. He loves chess, so we stopped in a tobacconist's shop that sold chessboards at a back counter. To my astonishment, the prices ranged from ten dollars to a thousand dollars. Jake chose wisely, picking a small magnetic travel set with plastic figures. Its price was $13.13.

Over lunch, Jake unwrapped the box as we waited for our sandwiches. As he set up all the pieces, I noticed his eyes were moist. He pointed to an empty place on the board and said, "I'm missing a bishop."

"That's okay," I said. "We can take it back. Lucky we opened it here instead of finding out about this all the way back home."

I tried to be upbeat, but I could see he was upset.

When the afternoon tests were over, I met with the doctors while he stayed in the waiting room. They said Jake had an "anxiety disorder" and then they used a term I had never heard before. They said he was "exquisitely sensitive." This meant that not only was he subject to extreme feelings, but he was also physically sensitive to the things that don't bother most of us. I knew that his mother had to cut the tags out of the back of all of his shirts, and I had seen him balk at keeping the baseball glove on his hand when he played the outfield. The doctors said they would be sending a thorough report to his mother shortly.

Jake seemed fine when I rejoined him, and his first words were, "Are we going to get the bishop now?"

The tobacconist did not have an extra piece for the set, and Jake looked at me and said, "I almost thought I was going to get a chess set."

"Oh, you are, Jake," I said. "We'll just choose another one. Let me see that one," I said to the clerk, and he held out another magnetic board, as small as the first. The pieces were very squat and ugly. The king looked like someone had dumped a bowl of spaghetti on his head.

We looked at set after set, but there was something wrong with all of them. Jake needed a travel set and they didn't have a decent one in my price range. Then he saw a carved board that folded up into a case. The pieces fit perfectly into the cover of the wooden case, making it portable. It was also expensive: forty-two dollars. The clerk and I had become friendly by this time, and he tried to convince Jake of the merits of the ugly, cheaper set for the sake of my wallet. He put the pieces on it and held the board upside down.

"Look how strong the magnet is," he said, waving the board. "They don't fall off."

"I still think I like this one," Jake said, pointing to the wooden set. "If it's all right." At seven, he was not aware of the price.

"Okay," I said. "We'll take it."

Jake jumped in the air.

"The boy has good taste," the clerk said to me as he took my receipt from the morning and looked at it. "Thirteen thirteen," he said, "It *was* unlucky."

Jake and I stopped for dinner on the way home. In the diner, Jake opened the set and arranged the pieces. Even in the fluorescent light that reflected off the Formica table, the board looked deep and burnished, like something from an earlier age, like something from the set of *Masterpiece Theater*. I pleased myself by thinking that Jake would always remember going to a tobacco shop and buying a chess set. There was something gently masculine about it as well as something antique.

Staring down, Jake said, "Mr. Skoyles, when I think I have a chess set like this, I feel like I'm going to cry." He had a big sentimental smile on his face and his eyes sparkled.

I felt like I was going to cry too. Jake got out of the booth and put his arm around me and I squeezed him.

It was a day I learned a new term, "exquisite sensitivity," and I thought it was too bad in some ways that one boy got such a big share of it when more of it could be spread around. But then I thought: I bet Jake will do that to the people he meets, make them just a little more thoughtful and sensitive to each other. As being with him had helped make me feel, at least for that day, and I hope longer.

All of Me

A FEW YEARS AGO I went to a concert by an elderly songwriter, Gerald Marks. He wrote songs in the twenties and lived and worked in that part of New York City known as Tin Pan Alley.

A small, jovial fellow in his late seventies, he played the piano and talked for almost three hours about his songs. He said it was a tough business, writing songs, and harder than that was selling them. He said you needed luck.

His biggest hit was "All of Me," which you might have heard. It's a wonderful, sentimental song about loss, but he said no one wanted to buy it. He played it in every music company's office around Times Square, where every executive refused it. Here he was with the best song he ever wrote, and no one would buy it.

Discouraged, he was sitting in a bar one evening when Belle Baker, the popular singer, walked in with some friends. Marks knew her slightly and asked if she'd listen to his song.

When he played it, she began to weep uncontrollably.

"That's my song," she said. "That's my song."

A few weeks later, she went into a recording studio and

cut the record. It became one of the biggest hits of the year. It's still recorded today.

Marks said that he ran into Belle years later, and she invited him up to her apartment in New York. They began to talk about old times.

He thanked her again for doing his song.

"You seemed to be the only one to appreciate it," he said.

Surprised, she said, "Didn't you know what happened the month before you played that for me?" Then she told him how her husband had been killed in a car crash, and the night she ran into Marks was the first time she had been out of her house. That's why the song moved her so deeply.

It's a sad story of loss and it's a tender story of love, but it's also an odd story of coincidence. Mainly, though, it's about people and how their lives intersect. You never know, when you're talking with someone, what they may have just gone through.

Marks ended his concert on a happy note. At the evening's close, he said that one song of his sold 50 million copies. A song called "If It Doesn't Snow on Christmas." He asked the audience if anyone ever heard of it. No one had. Then he said it was the B-side of a song he didn't write, "Rudolf the Red-Nosed Reindeer," and he said he doubted anyone ever turned that 78 over and played his song, but he made money on it every time a copy of "Rudolf" was sold.

It was true: he said you needed luck, and you do. But you also have to know how to write about the human heart well enough for a grieving woman to say, "That's my song."

The Collector

MY FRIEND Walter Michaels is a high school teacher who collects books. Most of us have our bookcases and our shelves filled with books we pick up here and there. We even lug around some books we've had since childhood.

But Walter is different. He collects books seriously. His library takes up a room in his house, all of it alphabetized, and most of the books are signed by the authors. Some of the books are wrapped in foil, and others are sealed in Ziploc bags. In other words, Walter is a nut about books. Worse, his study serves as the guest room for me during each visit, and I have to face the enormity of his obsession as I fall asleep each night and again when I wake up in the morning.

Whenever I'm on the road and there's a chance I'll meet a writer, Walter asks me to have a book signed. This can be embarrassing. One time, at Southern Methodist University, when the distinguished poet Elizabeth Bishop came to speak, he urged me to have her sign a book. Her arrival in Dallas was such an event that all the books were sold out. I finally found one copy but the bookstore owner was reluctant to sell it to me. "It's my last copy," he said. I was touched by his affection, and he finally did let it go.

Because I was teaching at the college, I was invited to dinner with the poet. After dinner, she read her poems, and students and teachers formed a long line in front of her, waiting to have her sign their books.

An elderly woman, she sat quietly, and politely asked each person his or her name as they stood before her.

I wanted the book signed to my friend, but to say so seemed to me to be verging on rudeness, as if I did not care enough to have it signed to me personally. The others in line carried several volumes, reverentially.

We had been introduced at dinner, but I was sure she would not remember my name, as there were over a dozen of us at the table. Still, I struggled with what to say as I approached.

Getting up the courage to do this favor for my friend, I stood before her and, when she asked my name, I said, "Walter." She had not remembered, of course, and bent her head to sign the book—but in all my worry about the poet, I had forgotten about my colleagues and students, who spun around and did double takes on hearing my new name. I blushed as I took the book from her, vowing that this would be the last humiliation I would endure for my friend and his hobby.

But to Walter, this awkward moment would have been nothing compared to the experience he had with the great South American writer, Jorge Luis Borges, who happens to be blind.

During one of my visits to his house, Walter told me the

story while we sat in his study. Borges was giving a lecture that Walter attended. He had been collecting Borges' books for years, and had several rare first editions. He was thrilled by the prospect of having these signed by the illustrious writer. As he told the story, Walter walked over to the B section of his library and stroked Borges' volumes on their shelf, as if to make sure they were still there.

The story is that after Borges gave his talk, Walter joined the enormous line of admirers who waited to speak to the famous man. When he finally stood beside the podium, he said, "Mr. Borges, I have some books I would like you to sign."

Walter opened each volume to its front page, piled them one on top of the other as you do in a library check-out line, and placed them on the podium to be signed.

When Walter named the titles, Borges reacted passionately.

"These are very rare," he said. "You must know my work quite well."

Walter beamed and handed Borges his pen, first clicking its top so that the ballpoint would be extended and ready to write.

Walter stood back, thrilled with Borges' warm reception, and with the prospect of having his beloved books autographed.

And then it happened.

As Borges felt for the page of the first volume, and smoothed it away from the binding, he lifted the pen over the page and, instead of writing, he pressed the back of the pen with his thumb, thinking he was extending its point. Walter said his whole body lunged forward to stop him, but he couldn't bring himself to do it, folding instead into a vertical heap, unable to speak.

Borges then pointed the blunt end of the pen to the pages and signed his name with a flourish on each one.

Walter looked on, horrified, as no mark was made on the pages.

He watched as Borges signed book after book with the useless pen, taking enormous care. Finally he handed the stack back to Walter, with a satisfied smile.

Walter was trembling by now, and white, and he thanked Borges, took the books and sat down in the front row.

He explained what had happened to the man next to him, another book fanatic.

"I don't mean to sound disrespectful," the man said, "but he is blind, and you could get back on the end of the line again."

"I couldn't!" Walter protested.

"Yes, you could. Just don't say anything this time and he'll sign them all."

Walter got up and stood on line for another half hour and had the books signed over again—this time not saying a word about their rarity to Borges.

The night that he told me that story, I couldn't fall asleep. I began to wander around his study, looking at the books. Strangely, on one of the shelves, he kept a plastic toy rifle that shot Ping-Pong balls. Earlier in the day, he had been amusing his dog with it, firing the harmless balls into the air, which the dog gently snared in his teeth.

Then I found the section of his library devoted to his

teaching. He had several copies of the anthology he used and, in a corner, some rolled up maps and charts. On the floor was a box of condoms, purchased by the school for a sex education class, which Walter also taught. I picked one up and, for some reason I cannot explain, part-mischief, part-idleness, and part-silliness brought on by insomnia, I placed a condom into the barrel of the Ping-Pong ball gun, and finally went to bed and fell asleep.

I left the next day, and had dreams when I was home about the books, the blind writer, and bouncing Ping-Pong balls.

A few weeks later my phone rang.

"You idiot!!" Walter yelled, but he was laughing. "You idiot!"

"What's wrong?"

Then he told me about the condom and the Ping-Pong ball gun, which I had forgotten all about.

He explained that his landlady, a very prim and formal woman, had come to town and decided to visit her properties. She made an appointment with him and arrived accompanied by her sixteen-year-old daughter and the daughter's friend.

Walter and his wife showed them through the house, pointing out the usual things, how they used the screened-in porch, what they planted in the yard.

He said that when they entered his study and saw his wall-to-wall books, they gasped at their magnitude. He said he felt a little embarrassed, and to take the edge off their perception of him as a stuffy scholar, he grabbed the Ping-Pong ball gun and called for his dog.

When the dog romped into the room, ready to play, he lifted the gun, and from the barrel's tip, out fell the condom, wrapped in foil, shiny and bright, like a flat and floppy bullet. Walter was shocked, but he connected me immediately to the prank. The landlady was more shocked, not only by the condom, but by her daughter's response.

Simultaneously, the friend and the daughter shrieked.

The friend said, "What's that?"

But the daughter said, "Oh god!"

It proved a litmus test. The daughter knew what she saw, and the landlady knew the daughter knew. By the end of that day, I bet the friend knew as well.

Walter said that he did not sound convincing when he claimed he knew nothing about it, saying, "Oh, we have a friend who likes to play tricks on us." No, it doesn't sound credible.

Who knew what havoc my idle toying in a room full of books could cause? How could I have guessed that I could get into trouble in that quiet place? I touched the only thing that wasn't signed in that room and, in a way, I left a kind of signature myself.

Mr. Bass

WHEN MR. BASS, a neighbor of ours in his eighties, was taken to the hospital, my mother went to visit him. He had known my mother since she was a child, and had been a wonderful friend to her. He had taken her to baseball games, the circus, and even to a speakeasy when she was no older than ten. He had never married and he lived with his sister. My mother's father had died young, so she and Mr. Bass made a good match. But as the years went on, my mother had her own family and, as Mr. Bass stayed in his apartment all the time due to failing health, she hardly saw him.

At a newsstand outside the hospital, she bought an enormous number of magazines: *Time, Newsweek, Sports Illustrated, TV Guide, Popular Mechanics*, and more. There were two reasons for this: one was that she felt guilty about not seeing Mr. Bass more often. The second reason stems from the first: she had no idea now what interested him.

When she got to the room number that Mr. Bass's sister had given her, she was shocked to see a gurney being rolled out of the room with an old man on it.

"Where are you going?" she asked.

"They're operating," the man said in a weak voice.

"Does your sister know they're operating?"

"No," he said.

After they rolled him away, she put the magazines on his bed and left.

At home, she dialed the sister and told her.

"They're not operating," the sister said. "It turns out he was just constipated."

"No," my mother said, "I saw them wheeling him into the operating room."

"I just hung up the phone with him," she said. "We're picking him up tonight. You must have had the wrong room."

It turned out my mother did have the wrong room, and the man she thought was Mr. Bass was a stranger, now richer with magazines from another stranger. At home, my mother explained that she couldn't recognize him after so many years. And the fact that he was lying down and not wearing his glasses didn't help.

"I thought he looked different," she said, "but I couldn't tell."

I always felt this incident was not really about Mr. Bass and my mother, but about not seeing someone at all, so that they disappear. My mother had her memories of Mr. Bass, but over the years they had detached themselves from the actual man living with his sister in the front room of an apartment. Instead, they should have added to their friendship as something to share and build on. He embodied an important past, no matter how feeble that body had become.

And what about the stranger on the gurney? There is the

real story: He is asked by a woman he doesn't recognize if his sister knows they are operating on him. What a question! Maybe he hadn't seen his sister in years. Maybe she lived across the country. Maybe my mother's question led him to call his sister after a long estrangement. Or maybe he was too medicated to remember, and he found the gift of magazines mysteriously left on his bed when he returned.

When I think about Mr. Bass and my mother, and even the mysterious sister created in this story only through speculation, I want to pick up the phone. I want to call someone I laughed and joked with years ago. And when I do, my friend is back, and it's the years that disappear.

Opposites

I WAS TWENTY-SIX when I started my first teaching job, and I had good classes. But in one section was an impossible student. It was a freshman English class at a university in Dallas, and the students were mostly hardworking, except for Steve. He never brought a book, paper, or pen, but just sat smirking while I talked. He came to class in a tuxedo, just back from a night on the town. I had to ask him to stop whispering several times throughout the hour. And then he would hiccup loudly.

Soon I had a dream about him: he was twenty feet tall and I looked up at him, up at the vast expanse of his ruffled shirt and cummerbund.

When I woke up, I asked myself: What do I feel about this student? Could I be afraid of him, to have dreamed of him as a giant? The dream troubled me for days.

Coincidentally, I was reading Carl Jung's autobiography, *Memories, Dreams, Reflections*. A few weeks after my dream I read about one of Jung's that fascinated me. He was treating a prostitute and couldn't seem to help her. Then one night he had a dream about her where she was standing on top of a mountain and he was staring up at her.

When Jung woke, he knew immediately what his dream meant. He said to himself: the dream is the opposite of what you really feel, it makes up for your conscious attitude. All along, he said, he had looked down on this woman because of her profession. He had not realized that he had adopted a superior moral attitude. When he admitted it, to himself as well as to her, they made progress and he was able to foster a breakthrough in her treatment.

I thought about this. I realized I had looked down on Steve for his cavalier attitude and also because I had heard him bragging about his conquests and seen him tearing out of the student parking lot in an expensive sports car. It also occurred to me that maybe I envied him a bit, having come from a generation of college students who favored workshirts and army jackets over formal wear. And perhaps now I was feeling the poorer for it.

We talked in my office, and when I mentioned this, all the glitter fell from him, and I saw him as a human being. I began to treat him differently, and he began to pay attention to the subject and to even join in the discussions.

YEARS LATER, I went back to Dallas and was in a restaurant when I saw Steve again. He was still in a tuxedo, surrounded by women. He came over to me, friendly as could be. We had a drink together and talked about the class.

"I was a real pain in the ass," he said.

"You were, but I think I brought out the worst in you."

"You know," he said, "that's true. You were so full of

morals and values and so was the stuff we read, that it made me the opposite."

"I held that tuxedo against you for a long time," I said.

Then he said something that shocked me: "And I held your one sports coat against you too!" He laughed and looked into his drink unselfconsciously.

I realized how I had appeared to him: the poor teacher with all the right values and none of the good things of the world. I think I might have seen myself like that too, without realizing it, as I drove by the bars and restaurants of Dallas, places with names like Daddy's Money that I was curious about but never entered. Once I even pulled into the parking lot of The Tabu Lounge but left, thinking I wouldn't fit in. I recognized now that I probably resented Steve's easy passage along Greenville Avenue's hot spots.

What had changed?

"I have two sports coats now," I joked, and we laughed.

"And I read more than you think," he said.

"Everything contains its opposite," the saying goes, and Steve and I sat there, expressing some skepticism about each other's way of life, and some envy too, on both our parts. But there is a pleasure in contraries, and by the admitting of opposites, our friendship was made.

The Stick

EVERYTHING I KNOW about being a father I learned from my wife. She had a child before we met and so when we had our own, she taught me what to do. The trouble is, sometimes I balked, and preferred the hard lessons of experience to those of a teacher.

One night, when our son Harry was a toddler, we took a stroll around the lake near our house. We had just finished dinner, and it was one of those cool autumn evenings when you welcome a change of season. As we walked, Harry picked up a small twig and waved it around as he walked. My wife immediately took it from him and he cried.

"Let him have the stick," I said.

"You don't let kids have sticks. They fall and poke their eyes out."

We resumed our walk, Harry wobbling ahead of us. With his diapers under his long pants, he waddled along like the ducks he chased, while I wondered about what my wife had said.

Chilly, she went back to the house for a sweater.

Harry picked up another stick and began waving it happily toward the ducks, the lake, the sky, absolutely enchanted with his new power. I let him walk with it.

We had gone no more than twenty feet when Harry tripped over a root and fell. He lay on the dusty path, kicking and crying. I ran up to him and saw the slight but very visible wound: the stick had cut a little red crease right up the center of his forehead, just as my wife predicted. Luckily, it had missed his eyes, and the scratch was thin and shallow.

A jogger ran up to us, eyed the stick, the crying child, the squatting father, and the forehead now divided by a crimson line.

"He fell on the stick," she said, bending over and looking at him. "It's not deep."

My wife returned just as the jogger left, saw Harry, and said, "You let him have the stick, didn't you?"

I admitted how stupid I had been. But for the rest of the walk, I thought that raising this boy will not always be so simple. And I still wondered, what were the chances that he'd fall on another stick?

Chang

MY FRIEND COOPER teaches American history at a public high school. He gets a raise each time he earns credit at a college, and he's been increasing his salary over the years by taking courses at night.

Tired of the usual government and civics courses, he signed up for one he thought would be easier than all the others: Chinese painting and poetry. What he found there changed his life.

The teacher was a Chinese painter, Chang Mo, but you just called him Chang. He spoke English badly but could make himself understood.

Cooper told me about him whenever we talked on the phone. After the course was over, he continued to see Chang and to go out to lunch with him. Chang's wife and children had been killed in China during the Maoist revolution, and Chang recently found his way to the United States, teaching at the University of Illinois. He was an accomplished painter and poet.

When I visited Cooper on his birthday, he arranged for me to meet Chang and I looked forward to it.

We met in his office, the walls absolutely bare, but books and scrolls of paintings were piled up on the floor and stacked onto furniture. He was very polite and Cooper and I sat there while he brought out the painting he made for Cooper's birthday, a surprise gift. It was a beautiful brush and ink drawing of a mountain dotted with trees, and Cooper was taken aback by the generous gesture.

Mistaking his stunned appreciation for disappointment, Chang said, "Oh, you wanted birds in it!" and he took a brush and made some quick strokes, birds appearing over the mountaintops.

WE HAD LUNCH at Chang's favorite place: the Sirloin Barn, a steak place where you pick up the steaks on trays as you go through the line. Chang ordered only a baked potato.

At the cashier, he asked us, "You be host or I be host?" and I decided to be the host since it was Cooper's birthday. Except for the fact of Chang's obvious generous nature and courtesy, I still had not seen the side of Chang that impressed Cooper as wise.

Then as we sat down, Chang began to talk. And he talked like an angel. I wanted to take notes on his theories and his high moral positions, which he held firmly and gave naturally, without pomposity. He said he felt there was too much negativity in the young students. He said they had to learn how to add to life rather than subtract from it.

To illustrate, he used haiku as an example. He said that people today are negative, they'll say:

Dragonfly
Pull off wings
Palm tree

but they should think:

Palm tree
Add wings
Dragonfly

A man walked by our table carrying a copy of *People* magazine, and our discussion turned to celebrities and fame and loneliness. Chang told this story: "One day there was a great archery contest in my village. People came from all over China to compete. The fields were full and everyone cheered. One man, Tang, shot the bull's-eye each time, and the contest lasted days. He never missed, and everyone applauded. Out of the corner of his eye, he saw a vendor, a man selling peanut oil, and he noticed that the vendor did not applaud. When the grand prize was awarded, and Tang received words of praise as well as riches from the Emperor, the vendor still did not applaud. Curious, Tang went up to him.

" 'Did you see me shoot this week?' Tang asked.

" 'Yes,' the vendor replied.

" 'And did you see me hit the target every time?'

" 'Yes, I saw that,' the vendor said.

" 'Then why didn't you applaud for me the way everyone else did?'

" 'Well,' the vendor said, 'You see my jugs of oil here.

Whenever someone comes to buy a cup, I pour a perfect cup each time, and no one applauds for me.' "

Chang ended the story with the words, "Everyone is important, not just celebrities. And everyone is equal."

Cooper is still in touch with him, and has sent me a list of proverbs from Chang:

> Do not insult the crocodile until you have crossed the river.
> It is better to struggle with a sick jackass than to carry the wood yourself.
> Do not throw stones at a mouse and break a precious vase.
> It is not the last blow of the ax that fells the tree.

It's amazing how two people meet, a high school history teacher with a family and an Asian painter without one, and how they become friends. I felt privileged to be the host at one of their meetings, in Illinois, in a sirloin barn, where everyone was important and everyone equal.

The Smoky Mountain Cage Bird Society

MY MOTHER'S FAMILY always kept pet birds. Hers was an Italian family, and if you've been to Italy and walked down the alleys of its cities and heard the canaries singing as they hang in their cages from open windows, you know how Italians love birds. My grandmother's canary flew around the house, out one window and back in the other, stopping on the terrazzo kitchen table to peck at a loaf of bread. He sang from morning till night, and his song would last a full minute at a time.

My uncle Pete raised canaries and would talk for hours about his special birds. He told me how the hen lays her first egg and then he removes it, substituting a plastic egg. The next day, she lays another and he substitutes another fake. He does this until she stops laying. Then he puts all the real eggs back into the nest and removes the fakes. This way, they all hatch at the same time, and there is no larger, dominant chick.

He had a special bird, an infertile hen named Grandma that loved to sit on eggs, although she never had any chicks of her own. Whenever a hen would not stay on its nest, he brought in Grandma.

He also had a parrot, an Amazon named Four Bucks. He

bought it right after the depression, when money was still scarce and he paid the then exorbitant sum of four dollars for it. He said he was going to teach it to do all kinds of tricks and antics, but all it did was screech and bite. My grandmother, Pete's mother, shook her head when he told her of his scheme and said, sadly, "Four bucks," and that's how it got its name.

So it's in my blood to love birds. I've had canaries that sang beautifully, finches that sounded like a New York apartment building doorbell (a sound that made my mother answer her door again and again during the winter she cared for them), cockatiels that could whistle Schubert, and parakeets that talked better than any expensive parrot, picking up the small, exasperated phrases uttered around the house, like "Work, work, work," "No way!" and "You monkey!"

I have three birds. The oldest is a canary named Primo, named after the Italian heavyweight boxer Primo Carnera. Then there is Jeep, an African Red-Bellied Parrot, and a little budgie, my son's bird, whom he named Chirp.

Primo just sings all day. Chirp talks a lot and flies from head to head. He looks best on the heads of distinguished visitors, as he slides down their foreheads and tries to preen their eyebrows. It's a sight that transforms the most stodgy professor into a helpless human being. Jeep is a clown who will hang upside down and put his head through his legs for attention. He greets us with "Good Morning" and says the appropriate farewell at night.

The worst sound he makes is that of the cat being stepped on, which made us realize that the cat must get stepped on a lot around here. The first time I heard it I leaped, thinking I had walked on the cat. Recently, he has taken up making the sound of the sliding glass door. One morning, I thought my son was playing with the door, as I heard it go back and forth, back and forth. But when I walked into the room, my son was reading. Jeep also makes the sound of my son sneezing: a child's *achoo*. He whistles the tune we use to call the cat, and when the cat comes, he looks over the top of his cage, and laughs, a wicked "heh, heh, heh."

A year ago I planned to add another bird, the bird that is known as the best talker of all, an African Gray Parrot. I studied them and learned everything there was to learn from books, finishing my studies with the conclusive volume, *The Gray Parrot*, by Wolfgang de Grahl. I learned how they could acquire 600 word vocabularies, and that in Germany, breeders would place them in households for two years before selling them. Later the birds would recite phrases and sing songs they overheard during that time.

Just a few weeks ago, a Gray was in the news because it was the first time a bird was being used as a witness in a trial. The bird's owner was murdered and when detectives investigated, they heard the bird cry the name of the accused, "Richard, no! No, Richard!"

A gray parrot sounded like an exciting addition to our lives.

The breeder called me when he had a baby ready. I went to see it and fell in love with the little ball of gray fluff. I held it and it was sweet and friendly. I came home and told my wife all about it. She went with me the next day. She, too, loved the bird, but while he was on her arm, he shook his feathers. As his wings flapped, a fine dander was released. The minute dust found its way to my wife's nose, and she had a huge allergy attack.

And so in one simple fluttery gesture, my year of reading and my study of Professor de Grahl's book flew out the window. Three is probably enough anyway.

IN THE SOUTH I joined a bird club with the fantastic name The Smoky Mountain Cage Bird Society. We met monthly, and there was a slide show at every meeting. After a few months, the librarian retired, and I was given the job. This meant I lugged an old orange crate of books from my house to each meeting, and kept tabs on a sign-up sheet.

I loved the people in the club. It was the first time I met serious bird keepers and breeders other than my relatives.

There were big strong men who could hold an hour-old bird and feed it with an eyedropper. There was Bill, an electrician who was a judge of finches and canaries. He lived with his sisters and kept birds in the basement. He had all kinds of prize winners and could flick his hand into the aviary and pull out any bird he wanted with great tenderness and accuracy. When I commented on this, he said, "I've caught a few."

There was Kyle, who had twenty orange-winged Amazons who wouldn't breed. "But when they do," he said, "just think what I'll have."

There was Joe, a pigeon racer. He hadn't been able to let his pigeons race for a year because a hawk had set up a nest near his house.

Every year we held a Swap and Sell in a hotel where we would rent tables to bird breeders and they would set up and sell and bargain with each other. There were raffles and food for sale. On our lapels, we wore long rectangular pins printed with our names and a little sketch of a bird's head and our club's name in caps: SMOKY MOUNTAIN CAGE BIRD SOCIETY.

At one event, I took the elevator up to our conference room with three guys from the club. Each of us wore his pin. Two girls got on along the way and rode up with us. Their eyes glanced at our pins. When they got off, they burst out laughing into their hands, and we laughed too. We were serious, but not that serious.

That year, the dean of the college where I worked wanted everyone to get involved in our community. At the end of the year, he sent a form around and asked what professional or community organizations we belonged to.

When I filled in: Librarian, Smoky Mountain Cage Bird Society, he called me and said he didn't want jokes.

"Come up and see my pin," I said.

I never heard from him again.

For which I thank the birds in the South and the birds in my life, which continue to fill our lives with song and parodies of ourselves at our best and our worst, and even our most private.

Suffering

MY NEIGHBOR just read a book about the way we die. He tried to get me to read it, but I declined, as I had already heard about each chapter from him each morning when we met on our way to work.

The book says there are seven ways to die, only seven. All other afflictions dwindle down to one of those seven. And there is no such thing as dying of old age. Again, it's one of the seven ways. He said the body is supposed to break down, it's not meant to last forever. In other words, General Motors did not invent the "planned obsolescence" that makes your car's parts give out after a certain period of time. They were just imitating Mother Nature's way with us.

It reminded me of a story about two very old friends. One complains to the other about all of his ills, and his friend turns to him and says, "You're not sick, you're just dying."

Since my neighbor read this book it's been hard to live next door to him. He knows everything about everybody's illnesses. I overheard him say to someone on the beach, "Oh, he had congestive heart failure?" Later, he said to me, "That means he won't live more than five to seven years." It can be hard to take.

He and his wife came over to watch a movie we rented last week. When the villain, a woman, killed a man by hitting him in the eye with her stiletto heel, and he lay writhing on the floor; the rest of us grimaced and my neighbor said very matter of factly, "I know how he's dying."

The funny thing is that he finds this comforting. "Knowledge is power," he says.

I've tried it. I bought a book with the very winning title of *Marriage: Dead or Alive!* It said marriage can be tough at times.

I remembered the Russian writer Chekhov's line: If you're afraid of loneliness, don't marry.

I bought another book on old age that I hoped would make me feel better. The bottom line was: you'll get old and it doesn't feel great but you should expect it.

I remembered my old and wonderful grandmother, wincing as she pulled herself out of her chair on her arthritic knees, and looking at me, saying, "Don't get old, Johnny."

I suppose there is a real comfort in these books, though none of them are explicit about it. The comfort is an odd one, that life is not supposed to be perfect and without pain. Every life has suffering in it. The trick is to learn to accept it.

Buddha said, "Life is suffering." The strength that comes from this acceptance is astounding. We stop complaining about pains and jolts we've suffered; we accept them as natural and we are joined with others in being the rule, not the exception.

Our things are supposed to break, yes, I guess I understand that, and when we include our bodies as well as our hearts in the formula we feel comforted in our union with the other frail beings on this planet.

Need

MAN MIGHT BE MOST HUMAN when he is most foolish. A few stories about bank robberies in this small town where I live certainly would serve as evidence of that theory.

A poor soul once robbed the town's only bank after a huge snowfall. The police arrived and followed his footsteps back to the door of his house, where he was sitting at his kitchen table, stacking the bills into envelopes. They were marked for the YMCA, the United Way, and other charities. He had written them out before the heist and for the return address he had printed: Mr. Robin Hood.

The worst story, though, has elements of folly as well as threatening violence. The robber approached the teller with a pen and pad in hand. After they exchanged greetings, he asked her how to spell the word "breathing." She spelled it for him, and he wrote it down. Then he handed her the note. It read: "Hand over $5,000 or you'll be breathing through a new hole in your face."

The teller recognized the man as a regular customer and inquired sympathetically as to why he needed the money. He said he and his wife decided to separate and he wanted half for her and half for himself, to get out of town.

The teller asked, "Doesn't your wife have an account with us?" And he said she did.

This is where the teller showed her savvy. She said, "Then why don't I just take her $2,500 and deposit it in her account?" The robber said that would be fine and left with his $2,500, telling her good-bye and thanks. He mentioned he was taking the next bus, which is where the police found him.

A surprising story about a bank robbery happened to a man named Willie, who lived in my parents' apartment building in New York City. This story shows the difference between small towns and gigantic cities, in terms of sophistication as well as the multitude of crime.

A few summers ago, there was a wave of bank robberies in the city. They were so numerous that the police had to stake out the banks they suspected might be next. So many police had to spend so many hours of overtime on this project that consumer groups started to protest, saying that the banks should provide their own security.

The numbers mounted, and in the month of July the papers reported that forty-five banks had been robbed. The record was forty-eight. As soon as the number of the record was released, detectives said they were sure the figure would inspire robbers to go for the mark. And sure enough, the next day there were two more hold-ups.

This is where Willie comes in. Willie has retired from his job, which was working at the counter of a store called Admiration Cigar, which sells magazines and newspapers. Willie is a very small fellow, originally from Brooklyn, and he once warned me about the city with these words, "Don't bunk into the wrong guys around here."

The day Willie's social security check came, he went to the bank to deposit it. After he handed the teller his paperwork, he was set upon by two security guards who tumbled poor Willie to the ground, handcuffing him.

It turns out that Willie had used a deposit slip he picked up from one of the bank counters, as all of us have done. But this slip was doctored by a prankster, who had written on the back, "This is a hold-up. Give me $20,000 in small bills." Willie just slid the slip over to the teller, who rang for security.

Willie was all right. He told me, when I met him in the elevator, that the bank had given him a $500 savings bond to make up for the rough tackle. They never found the prankster.

THESE ARE ALL STORIES of folly, but they all stem from need. I can't help but feel for the man depositing the stolen money for his wife. The prankster had a need too, but God knows what that was and how he filled it after the crime wave passed. He preyed on folly, on the public's interest in a wholly idiotic statistic. And the guy who left the trail in the snow had generous intentions. I bet that if you imagine yourself at your kitchen table, counting a large number of bills that came your way, you'd give some of it away, and I bet that names of individuals and organizations come immediately to your mind.

Americans give more money to the needy per person than the people of any other country. And we do it even when it might not be our own.

Patron Saint

I HAVE AN ENVELOPE in front of me. It's a blue envelope, printed with the address of the St. Jude shrine at the church of St. Catherine of Sienna. It has been returned by the post office, who has mistakenly stamped it with the words MOVED, NOT FORWARDABLE. The postmark is December 7, 1977.

I learned about St. Jude years ago, when I was a teenager. My Aunt Linda had asked me to go with her to New York Hospital to visit a friend. Because my aunt was on in years, she didn't want to go alone to the east side of Manhattan from Queens, where we both lived. On the way back, it rained. The shower became very hard as we reached the front of that church, St. Catherine of Sienna, so we ran in. St. Catherine's turned out to be the church where my Aunt Linda had been baptized early in the century. We met a priest in the back of the church who said he'd look her up in his records. My aunt is Italian, by the name of Bertolotti. The priest said they had two books in those days for recording births: an Irish book and an Italian book. She was correctly placed in the Italian book. Talk about filing systems!

In that church is a shrine to St. Jude, and that's where I

first heard of him. Holy cards are free for the taking there, and I lifted one out from the rack and read the prayer, the petition in which you ask for your favor. A brochure mentioned that St. Jude is known by several titles: The Patron of Lost Causes; The Patron of Hopeless Cases; The Patron of the Impossible. Who wouldn't be attracted to him? In this church he was Patron of Hopeless Cases. I felt sure I qualified and I knelt. I had many favors to ask. And many favors granted.

MY AUNT has been dead for years now. This card came to me, along with other things of hers at her death, and I have kept it. Inside is an "Enrollment Blank," which my aunt had mailed in with a dollar bill for an Annual Individual membership in my name, as a birthday present for me. But I never got enrolled because the post office turned it back. (Come to think of it, it wouldn't be a bad idea for the post office to adopt St. Jude as their patron as well!)

The dollar is still inside. How can I spend it? Besides, it seems like a rejection of my membership and I don't like that feeling. Next time I'm in New York, I'll visit St. Catherine's and slide it into the slot there in the rack of votive candles and light one for my aunt.

Cars

I GOT MY FIRST CAR in college and knew nothing about maintaining it. It was a Mercury Comet and it was a lemon. In the winter, it took forever to warm up, and I had to let it run for twenty minutes before I could go on the road without stalling.

The estimate to fix the problem was outrageous, so I figured I'd have to live with it. I'd start the car each morning and then go back into the house for another cup of coffee. When I wasn't at home, I'd sit in the car reading a book called *Great Letters of the World*, which I kept in the glove compartment.

Still, it was annoying and a waste of gas, and so one day at a yard sale when I found a thick manual about my car I bought it for a dollar. After hours of reading, I decided my problem was in the carburetor. I bought a rebuilt Holley double-barrel carburetor and put it in. Soon the car wouldn't start at all. After a whole Saturday of fiddling, I finally got the engine to turn over. But there was a major shortcoming, and the only way it would work was if I performed the following procedure every time I started the car: pump the gas pedal; get out and open the hood; unscrew the carburetor housing; flip the little lid back until it lay flat; close the hood; get back in the car and start the engine.

The Comet had another problem: it wouldn't start after it rained. I had to open the hood and spray a can of Wire Dyer onto the distributor cap. Then I'd close the hood, get back in the car and start the engine. Once, in the middle of a terrible rainstorm, I couldn't close the hood, the hinges were so stiff and rusty. While I struggled, the cap got wet again. I went back in the car, and the engine wouldn't start. Again, I opened the hood, sprayed the cap, and again, the hood buckled. Each time the car failed to start. In and out of the car I went in the pouring rain until I finally got the hood to slam.

My favorite car was a big Chevy Malibu with a V-8 engine. After a few years, it developed holes in the pipe of its exhaust system and made such boisterous noise that I was afraid to stay out late because I would wake everyone up when I came home. I went to Benny's Auto Supply where they suggested I do the job with Tiger Patch. Tiger Patch is a roll of tape, like duct tape, but cut into a gridlike design. It cost ninety-nine cents for a roll and I bought six rolls. I crawled under the car and wrapped the pipes, but I noticed that I was also missing a small section of pipe. I went back into the house a little dejectedly. When I opened the refrigerator to get a drink, I saw a six-pack of V8. The can looked to have the same circumference as my exhaust pipe, and when I got back under the car, it filled the gap perfectly. And the Tiger Patch worked. For a while at least.

A less successful venture took place when I junked that car. It died on my way to work and I had it towed to A. T.

Hopkins' Mobil Station. A. T. called me with the bad news: shot transmission. Eight hundred dollars to replace it, about four times the worth of the car, so I'd have to junk it.

I paid A. T. twenty-five dollars for towing the car. Now, he said, it would be another twenty-five dollars to tow it to my house, about two miles away. When A. T. saw that I didn't care for this predicament, he said, "Well, it still runs backward. You could back it home."

I started the engine and it did go backward. Now I faced another dilemma: when you're backing a car down the road for two miles, which lane do you use? I decided on the right lane and I made it home fine, with the exception of a few curves on hills. After all, we were in Black Mountain, North Carolina.

My wife met me and said she had called the only wrecker in town and that he was coming right over to take it away. He mentioned seventy-five dollars. Then I remembered I had filled my twenty-one gallon gas tank that morning: that alone was worth at least twenty-five dollars.

I decided to siphon the gas into the gas tank we kept for the lawn mower. But I had no siphon.

My daughter brought me a cheap transparent tube from her aquarium, and the sun set on that Friday evening with me kneeling on gravel as I bent behind the Chevy, holding down the license plate's spring mechanism with protected gas cap, sucking on a tube from the fish tank, getting several mouthfuls of gas, and finally giving up.

"The end of an era," my wife said as the car was yanked onto the wrecker, and I held the seventy-five dollars. I spent the next hour trying to get the taste of gasoline out of my mouth and I swore I would never touch the insides of a car again.

BUT I DID. One more time. And I remember that last time very well. It was two years later, in New York City, in autumn. My friend told me that I should check the strength of my anti-freeze, and that he had the gauge to do it. He brought over the little bulb connected to an eyedropper with four little balls floating in it. The problem was that the tube of the eyedropper, the three-inch tube that sticks on the end, came off when I was swishing it around the overflow bottle and fell in. I was sure it would melt and wreck my engine. I had another Chevy then, a Nova I was attached to. It was Sunday morning, when New York's streets are filled with people getting newspapers and pastries. They are off from work and they are interested in anything. Every passing stranger had a suggestion. There were the doomsayers who said the tube would cause big problems. There were the optimists who said it would just lay on the bottom. But I knew I would not rest until I got the tube out.

My friend went back to his apartment to get some tools. He came back with a pair of chopsticks, and that was the last time I worked on a car: leaning over the engine, balancing a pair of chopsticks on three fingers of my right hand and gently placing them into the mouth of the overflow bottle, dipping them in again and again, as into a bowl of chop suey, while a crowd gathered, each person holding a fat newspaper and a white bag from the bakery that gave off a wonderful fragrance, each happy to be entertained, and happier still when I pulled the tube out of the engine and held it high. Everybody cheered. I can still recall the chopsticks. And the name of the restaurant, the Dragon Seed, still burns before my eyes.

Frankie

MY PARENTS THOUGHT I should see the world, and so when I turned fifteen, they got me a summer job away from our neighborhood in Queens. My Aunt Linda arranged for me to work as a messenger in the mailroom of Paramount Pictures, where she worked then and where she would work for forty years.

It was a strange job, because it meant hanging around a mailroom with what my aunt would later call "unsavory characters," until I was sent out on an errand. My companions were often guys who ran numbers and sold drugs, although most of the boys were customers: they played the numbers, bought the drugs, and were general victims of schemes.

I did see the world, the underworld of small-time operators, and I guess that was worth something. There was really no other choice except to hang around our local park back home and play the radio very loudly.

I met some unforgettable people at Paramount. Some were the nieces and nephews of movie stars: Burt Lancaster's nephew worked with me. But most memorable were the waifs who passed through our doors, men the likes of which I had never seen before.

Frankie was the dearest to me. I met him when our boss went out early one day and the mailroom was in an uproar, yardsticks spilled across the floor and flailing everywhere.

As part of a continuing publicity campaign for Paramount's latest release, *Harlow* (a sensational life of the blonde bombshell, Jean Harlow) the advertising department ordered yardsticks with the Paramount logo. They were supposed to resemble thermometers, red ink soaring past large black numbers reading "103 degrees," showing how Carroll Baker's performance could make an audience's temperature rise. We received them by the boxful, as we received the first of everything. The department that came up with the idea, the artist who designed it, the executive who produced it, none of them held the finished product until it had passed through our hands. We were the lowest of the low in the company and yet we had this power. One of the boys, Phil, pointed this out to me, proudly, and with the appropriate sense of irony: the rest of the company had to wait for us to deliver what they created. Everyone in the mailroom was aware of this, and it gave us a sense of importance. "Rush" envelopes, which were made of a hot pink paper, were opened and checked for their urgency. Phil once found one containing a recipe for crabmeat casserole, considered it thoughtless, and shelved it for days.

I actually saw Frankie for the first time when these yardsticks arrived though I had heard about him. He was standing near the pneumatic tubes which zoomed heavy capsules containing letters to the receptionists' desks above. Every so often a receptionist would drop the container back down and it would land in a deep trough of rags. It was not a good place to stand, and I wondered why this man leaned so close.

Frankie worked for the Fleet Messenger Service and wore glasses so large and thick they looked as if they came from a novelty shop. His head bobbed when he spoke, and he smiled constantly, as if expecting you to get a joke he just told. He was well known in our mailroom for what our boss called "getting stuck"—he would sway from side to side, holding his black straw fedora in both hands, just below his waist, and couldn't stop swaying. When this happened, we were under orders from the boss to yell, "Okay, Frankie!" which roused him on his way.

Frankie could also get trapped in a phrase, repeating it uncontrollably. When I went up to him, to suggest he move away from the tubes, he began talking about racehorses, saying, "Some run good in the rain. Called mudders. They run good in the rain. Mudders don't mind the mud. The rain don't bother them. They like the rain. Called mudders." One of the boys walked by and said, "Enough, Frankie," and he stopped immediately, smiled, and pulled a stick of gum from his pocket, offering it.

Paramount's messengers looked down on Frankie and other runners from small messenger companies like Fleet, since most of them were considered mental cases or alcoholics. All were unskilled and knew nothing but the routes through the city they followed over and over.

It was funny how the yardstick brought out the personality of each person in the mailroom. Mario, the guy who worked the dumbwaiter and who was a survivor of the wreck of the *Andrea Doria*, walked back and forth considering the yardstick, then placed it near the packing shelf. He said, "The UPS man can use it, he's always measuring." I stood my yardstick in a corner near the coatrack, to bring home to my mother. Some of the messengers were fencing, and one began to carve up the wood with a long switchblade.

Frankie looked around, the same constant smile on his face, and Phil told me to give him one. I held it out, but he just swayed. Mario made the sound of an alarm clock in his ear, and Frankie took the yardstick.

We walked out together, Frankie saying, "Thank you! Oh, thank you very much! Thanks! Thanks a lot!" I yelled, "You're welcome!" which stopped him, and he turned brightly, and said, "Now I can see how much I weigh."

It is shocking to have a man look openly into your face and say such a thing. It is a greater shock when you are a boy. Frankie's face, lit for a second with the thrill of the gift and, more, with the idea of how to use it, was pure. I was becoming an expert at interpreting tone, for in this room I had heard the tones of irony, ridicule, hatred, disgust, self-disgust, envy, and despair. I had already been scoffed at that summer for taking a mocking remark to heart. Frankie's statement was shocking in that it forced me to return to my former way of believing what was said, and yet I found it unbelievable.

Touched and sorry, I said, "No, Frankie, it shows how tall you are."

"Oh," he said, holding the yardstick upright at his side and standing at attention, "I'm taller."

You were taller, Frankie, taller than most of the world that looked down on you.

A Mentor

I HAVE ALWAYS been jealous of people who have mentors, as I have envied people who can name a book that changed their lives. I can never exactly point to a single book, just a mass of thoughts, feelings, and details in books I've read. They've all added up to a complex of ideas and notions that I've had over the years. One author doesn't stand apart from the others. There are no giants. In fact, I love some pipsqueaks in the world of books. One of my favorite writers was the sportswriter Jimmy Cannon. Every once in a while he'd write a column entitled "Nobody Asked Me, But . . ." a list of one-liners, geared to upset the establishment, and almost always not about sports. Here are some I recall:

Airline hostesses seem to be thinking about something else when they talk to me.
I find that guys who talk with cigarettes in their mouths are seldom modest.
Even when I'm late for an important appointment, I'll stop to read chalk writing on the sidewalk.

Low art to be sure, not by any means "politically correct," but memorable for thirty years.

In the same way, I've learned a lot from a lot of people, some of whom are mentioned in this book. They were all mentors in a way, even if they did not hold positions of prominence or prestige. But I always envied my colleagues, neighbors, and the strangers I'd meet on planes, who could point to a true "mentor," the person who had guided them along, shown them the ropes, and whom they looked to for advice. Sometimes this was a teacher, but more often it was a person in business who taught them something.

I had never had a person like that in my life, until I met Anne Stevens.

Anne Stevens worked at a college in North Carolina with an enrollment of less than four hundred students. I happened to work there at the same time, just when she became Dean. Anne was in her sixties, a very quiet and calm woman. At meetings, you'd forget she was there, until she piped up with one comment that solved the thing we'd been going round and round on.

Anne was the woman who officially hired me, and with whom I was to negotiate my salary and benefits. We met in her small office, and she held a sharpened pencil and a pad. She told me what the salary would be and the benefits. This school did not pay much. I had made more money at the job I had just left, at a well-known college in New York, but people did not come here for money. It was an idealistic place, where students did not pay room and board fees. Instead, each student worked fifteen hours a week on a different "crew," and in this way they maintained the campus' entire physical plant. It was a wonderful system. Having the students in charge of the grounds led to great benefits; for instance, we had no vandalism. If one student were to break a window, it was another student who had the task of fixing it. Also, students who emptied wastebaskets each day garnered a certain appreciation of labor, something the Ivy League experience rendered only in the abstract.

So I was happy to be there, low salary and all. But Anne was willing to give all of us a little more, to help us get by, as long as the college could afford it.

At one point in our conversation, she said, "I see you're taking quite a pay cut to come here."

"I knew that," I said. "I'm not here for the salary."

We discussed personal plans, and when she found out my wife and I had a baby on the way, she seemed surprised and looked back at her legal pad.

"I suppose you want to live on campus," she said.

"No," I said, "I'd rather live in town." Though the campus was beautiful, I did not want to live where I worked. I always liked driving away from the day's work, leaving it behind me. I recall the old baseball pitcher, Bob Lemon, talking about not taking the game home with him. Lemon said, "I always left it at some bar along the way." I didn't leave my worries at a bar, but let them fly out the car windows as I cruised home.

"Are you sure?" she said. "It's beautiful here."

"Yes," I said. "My wife might get a job in town and I'd rather be there."

"I think you'd like the campus," she insisted.

"I do like it," I said, "and maybe in a few years we'll change our minds."

"You mean you'd like to live here in the future?"

I had no idea where this conversation was going, and yet it was not pressuring that she was doing. We were both smiling the whole time.

"Someday, maybe," I said.

"Just say that, what you just said, that you'd like to live here."

"But I don't!" I said, laughing.

"Trust me," she said. "Just say it. Between us. To see how it sounds."

"Okay," I said, worn down. "I'd like to live here."

She looked down at her pad.

"That's too bad," she said, "because there aren't any houses available. And when we can't honor a request, we have to give you an additional $250 a month housing allowance to find your own place off campus."

That was Anne Stevens, generous, canny, and wise.

ONE TIME, when I was in her office, she opened her mail. As she read to the end of a long letter, she found a favor was requested. She turned to me and smiled, saying, "When you write someone for a favor, ask them right away, in the opening paragraph. Otherwise, it looks like the first part is false."

Another time, overhearing me on the phone with a friend, she said, "Whenever I have good news, I like to keep it until the end of the conversation, and that way they can tell all the things that happened to them first. If you give them your big item right away, it stops the conversation and you don't hear the little things you love about them, because they'll think they're insignificant compared to your news."

At graduation, a bunch of sailors came up to her to thank her for some good things she had done for them. They were going back to the Navy, and she wanted them to keep up their habits of reading and writing. She said, "Remember, that piece of paper," and she pointed to their diplomas, "just means you've sighted land. It doesn't mean you've gotten there yet."

Anne and I spent a lot of time in each other's offices. She used to come to mine to borrow my cigarette lighter for the Lucky Strikes that eventually caused her death. I didn't smoke, but kept a disposable lighter in my drawer, where I found it when I moved in.

She appeared at crucial times, asking for the lighter, saying she had run out of matches. I never understood the coincidence between her appearances and some tough times I was having, but by the time she left, the office full of smoke, I had always poured my heart out and she had given me advice.

CANCER TOOK HER quickly. One day she mentioned she was going in for a checkup, and within the week she was dead. I went to the service at our chapel, where members of the community stood up and told their recollections: how she signed every letter, "Cheers"; how she arranged for women's teams to be taken seriously on campus; and other warm memories. I had never been to a funeral of this kind and I could not speak. The tears were running down my face and I cried as I had not cried in years, as I have not cried since.

I kept the Bic lighter in my drawer, and sometimes I'd place it on the top of my desk. I felt superstitiously that it would draw Anne back to my office. I realized I was doing something primitive Indians did, which she had told me about. She said that a group of English anthropologists were studying a tribe in South America, and when their work was done, they left. The Indians were glad to be left alone, but as the years passed, their children heard tales of their visitors. As the legends of their gifts grew, the children decided to entice them back.

To attract them, the Indians built a long and wide path, like a runway, and placed lanterns high along its sides. They hoped this imitation landing strip would bring the big planes they had heard about, not realizing, of course, that it was usually the people in the planes who built the strip. I guess they felt the planes would just descend and bring them gifts when they spotted the rough runway.

And when I took out my lighter, I know I hoped Anne would reappear at my office door, leaning against the doorframe, drawn there by the lighter, to give me the gifts of her presence and advice, and in the truest sense, her wisdom and her love.

The Hunting Jacket

MY FRIEND TOM visited me in New York one summer, taking the train from upstate. I met him at Grand Central Station, and he was wearing a black and red hunting jacket, a furry thing, with large checks. I teased him about it, and we left for a bar called the Guv'nor. Tom drank a lot in those days and developed an immediate but bashful crush on the waitress. He was a polite fellow, and his affection remained unspoken.

Tom wanted to go to another bar, a bar he had read about that spring. There was an article in the *Daily News* about a shooting there, and he wanted to see what the place looked like. He was thinking about moving to the city, and he wanted to see just how bad it could be and whether he could handle it. He took the clipping from his wallet and asked if I knew the place. It was named Devlin's Eerie Bar, and I said I didn't know it, but that I knew where it was. The article described an argument over bets on a football game and how a patron was shot repeatedly in the chest.

"I think it should be okay in the daytime," I said. "But I don't want to go there at night."

We walked over to Lexington Avenue and went in. The

place was empty except for a couple arguing in a booth. Tom kept putting money in the jukebox to drown them out, but whenever a song ended, we heard snatches of their conversation, like, "Go ahead, keep comparing me to Dave," and, "It goes deeper than that."

The bartender gave us our drinks and then went back to dunking his mop into a steaming bucket and, to our surprise, lightly brushing the ceiling. Ammonia water dripped and ran down his arms.

"What a night last night," he said.

"What happened?" Tom asked, enthused.

"The guys started doing tricks. You heard of O'Malley? He's one of the mayor's deputies, something like that. He broke a broom over the back of his neck. Then Paretti says he can drive a nail into the bar with the palm of his hand. I get him a nail and he stands it right here on the bar. The crowd's leaning over his shoulder. He asks for a handkerchief, and I give him a Hav-a-Hank here. He drapes it over the nail, raises his palm way over his head and slams it down. *Boom!* The nail goes right through his hand and blood flies up to the ceiling."

He went back to dabbing at the splotches. The couple had stopped arguing to listen and they too looked up at the ceiling.

In the quiet, Tom seemed to get his bearings. I felt he was picturing himself sitting here, or in a place like it, having made the move to New York City.

Just then the door flew open and the room filled with quick explosive bursts. Before I could turn, I was knocked off the stool. I crashed to the ground, my heart pounding, and crawled and scrambled as fast as I could toward the back room.

But first, I had to get out from under Tom, who had flung me down and thrown himself on top of me, in order to protect me.

The next thing I knew we were standing in the kitchen, listening for movement and peeking out from the swinging door. The bartender was laughing. He held the door to the street open and waved us over. In the vestibule, little curlicues of blown up paper littered the floor, the remains of a pack of firecrackers.

"Just kids," the bartender said, "getting ready for the Fourth."

I was touched by my friend's selflessness in his panic, and I thanked him.

"I don't think I'll move here after all," he said later. "It's too noisy."

HE CAME BACK in the fall and we met again at the Guv'nor. I got there first and when he came in the waitress remembered him. Before he could order, she said, "Double Scotch, right?"

Blushing, Tom said, "I guess you remember me because not many people wear a hunting jacket in New York in the summer." I was sorry I had teased him about the jacket. He had taken my joking to heart.

"No," she said, turning away. "Not many people drink as much Scotch as you do."

Tom doesn't drink anymore. But he did move to New York, and the city treated him more kindly when he walked through it sober. When a drunk walks into a city, guided by a drunk, and looking for drunks, he finds them. He finds fear, violence, and disappointment as well. Still, Tom came through when he thought we were going to be written up in gory head-lines in the *Daily News*. Now we toast the folly of the old days, although the glasses we raise are filled with club soda.

An Old
Steel Hammer

IN THE DAYS when skyjackings were rampant, I was stopped and frisked at La Guardia Airport. And I guess it was my fault.

A favorite uncle of mine had died, my uncle Pete, the one who had driven me to my first day of college. I flew up to New Jersey from the South where I had been living. Pete worked as a hatcheck clerk at the Sands Casino in Atlantic City. He enjoyed life and was always laughing. I loved to hear him talk happily about the big tippers.

"Wayne Newton," he'd say, "Boom! One hundred dollars!"

Uncle Pete took me to my first baseball game at Yankee Stadium when I was a kid, treated me to lunch at the Automat by handing me a fistful of nickels, and bought me a tie pin and money clip at Brooks Brothers. I had never seen these places, because I grew up in the borough of Queens, and I've always been thankful to him for showing them to me.

After the funeral, an aunt who also served as executor of the will invited all the relatives to his apartment for coffee. As he was single, having divorced years back, we were invited to take any personal things we wanted. One of my cousins chose the bureau; another, the brass bed. At the time, I lived in a very small furnished apartment and couldn't fit anything more into it. I decided to look for something small and I rummaged through his kitchen's junk drawer. There I found it: a hammer that belonged to my grandfather, which my uncle Pete and I had used on our front steps when I was a kid. It was a beautiful hammer made entirely of steel and not more than eight inches long. The end of it had a groove for pulling bent nails out of wood. I still have it today. Imprinted on its side is: Bridgeport Iron Foundry 1914, and also its bizarre name, THE HOOKER, because of the split handle made for yanking out bent nails.

Pete and I, a city uncle and a city boy, used to tap acorns open and find the worms, which we put into jars with food to make them happier, we thought.

I was delighted with the hammer and then I found another tool which brought back great memories: an ancient ice pick my grandmother used to flick away at a block of ice. It had a wooden bulblike handle and a long steel prong. It was a piece of history, of this country, as well as of our family.

I told my cousins and aunt that these were what I wanted. They generously tried to press other things on me: an antique tea chest, a rocking chair, some crystal. I said that I couldn't take those things on the plane, and stuffed the tools into my bag, wrapping them in some undershirts. After another cup of coffee, I left for the airport while the others sorted things out.

I whisked through the check-in point and was ready to pick up my bag on the other side of the x-ray machine when two policemen grabbed me. They held my arms and the clerk at the conveyer belt asked what I had in my bag.

"A steel hammer and an ice pick," I said, and they looked at each other.

"I just came from a funeral," I continued. "My uncle died and these belonged to him."

My explanations were absolutely idiotic and they sounded worse as I went on.

"My uncle worked in Atlantic City, for a casino," I said. "I was up for his funeral." Suddenly I realized I had painted the picture of a hit man for the mob, if they believed that story at all.

The clerk took out the ancient tools and stared at them, disbelieving. They were too old to look menacing, yet by appearing so out of place they also looked guilty of just being themselves, old-fashioned tools in a place of high technology.

The cops took me over to a wall, and did what they called "patting me down," looking for other weapons. After I told them I was a teacher, and showed them my identification, they said, "Okay, you can take them on the plane, but we're keeping them up front until you get off." I guess they thought I might hijack the plane with a hammer and an ice pick. But I guess they've seen stranger things.

I USED the ice pick last week, to put a new hole in my son's belt. And my son and I used the hammer on the stoop, nailing a little square block to a long board, naming it a "submarine." The handle on the pick is beginning to crack, but the steel will last and last, as do the memories of Uncle Pete and the trouble his tools gave me, which would have made him laugh.

The Pumpkin Contest

ONE SUMMER, the clerk at Fairview Nursery gave me a free packet of seeds at the checkout line. The label read, GIANT PUMPKIN SEEDS, and I showed them to my six-year-old son and we both smiled in anticipation. The clerk told us to plant them and to make sure we came back in October, around Halloween, when the nursery gave away prizes for the biggest pumpkins.

On the other side of our backyard fence was a big incline, a forty-five degree angle full of weeds, blackberry brambles, and huge inkberries. I never thought anything would come of the seeds, so we took them and simply tossed them over the fence into a pile of old grass clippings, and we turned the hose on. Then we forgot about them.

A few weeks later, when my son hit the Whiffle ball over the fence, I went back there and was astounded to see some sturdy-looking vines crawling along the ground and ready to flower. We had never planted anything before, and it was thrilling. Then we watched every day.

Some mean-looking weeds seemed as if they might stunt our pumpkins' growth by blocking the sun, but the vines kept growing. Another kind of vine tried to wrap a choke hold on our pumpkin vine, but the pumpkin won out and the other just crinkled and dried up. Then little pumpkins began to appear, about a dozen of them. And it seemed that the vines grew about a foot a day.

Harry and I walked back and stared at them. At first this had been a lark, but now we cared. We would have been disappointed if something happened to these pumpkins.

One pumpkin in particular, growing right next to the fence, began to widen enormously. Others followed, but this one was outstretching all the rest. A vine climbed our neighbor's fence and he remarked that one of our pumpkins was over at his place. We told him he could have it. Another vine climbed down the hill and then up a tree, so that a pumpkin was growing as it hung from a limb. It sagged like a water balloon but continued to grow. These were tough and resilient vines, and we were totally engrossed by them.

The special pumpkin continued to grow. It got laughably large. At this time, a fellow was patching our roof, and when he took a break I saw him standing next to the fence, shaking his head. When I went out to chat with him, he said, "I wondered when I was up there if that could really be a pumpkin. It must weigh eighty-five pounds." I guessed he had to be right, and we marveled at it in the morning, again in the evening when I came home from work, and once more after dinner. It was like a new pet.

Soon October rolled around and for the first time we thought: could this pumpkin possibly win the contest? Should we enter it?

Of course we should! We looked forward all the more to each day.

On the Saturday morning of the contest, it was my job to cut the pumpkin from its vine and get it into the car. We had patted ourselves on the back for our cavalier manner of tossing the seeds over the fence and reaping great rewards. Now it was time to learn how planning might have made life easier.

Only one gate led to the other side of the fence where the pumpkin grew, and that one gate was all the way at the other end of the property line. I could climb the four-foot fence, but there was no way I could lift the pumpkin over it. So I had to get a wheelbarrow and go through the gate and across the entire width of the yard, over two hundred feet on a forty-five degree angle through blackberry brambles. I did it and arrived at the pumpkin scratched, bleeding, and sweaty. Lifting the pumpkin was no small matter either, and I finally got it into the wheelbarrow. Then I made my way back, dreading the pumpkin would roll out and down the hill. I was a total wreck by the time I got the thing next to the car door.

About fifty entries were being weighed at Fairview Nursery, and when two employees carried our pumpkin toward the scale, everyone oohed and aahed. It weighed 112 pounds and we were in first place. A few minutes later a truck pulled up with a pumpkin twice the size of ours, and then another truck with one almost as large as that.

I was surprised at how happy my son was with third prize. When a man asked me, "What did you do, clip the flowers off the vine and let that one take all the juice?" My son answered before I did: "We just threw the seeds over the fence!" and I nodded in agreement. My son got a one hundred dollar savings bond as a prize.

I talked with the men who had the largest pumpkins. One said he used fish fertilizer as well as all kinds of expensive nutrients. His wife said, "He went crazy over that pumpkin," and rolled her eyes. But you could tell she was pleased. It was an admirable job, but it reminded me of a white elephant.

Do you know where the expression "white elephant" comes from? When the king of Siam took a dislike to a member of his court, he gave him a beautiful white elephant. The upkeep of such a beast was tremendous, so to care for it properly meant ruin. On the other hand, not to care for it properly also meant ruin, because neglect would be an insult to the king. So it might have been with pumpkins, but luckily Halloween rolled around.

We placed the pumpkin at our driveway entrance. It was great to see it on the cement, where it was clear of weeds, and even to see its ugly side, the white and splotched place where it had been touching the ground. We loved every bit of it.

On Halloween eve, we carved a big face.

The giant pumpkin had been one of those rare gifts that arrive in spite of doubt and that makes them all the more miraculous.

Evidence

DO YOU REMEMBER when you were a kid, the first time you realized that when you did something wrong it would be found out? There's a period of innocence when you are sure that only you know what you did, and the big shock comes when the crime is traced back to you.

I have two distinct memories of my discovery of the existence of evidence. The first occurred when I was five, and I know that because we lived in Connecticut then, and I can picture the house and the porch and the wrought iron railing in the background. In front of me is my arm, the sleeve of a blue wool sweater. It is autumn and my mother has been trying to cure me of the disgusting habit of wiping my nose on my sleeve. I had promised earlier in the week that I would never do it again. Coming in from the cold, she met me on the porch and asked me if I kept my promise while I was playing tag in the driveway. As it was a habit and I had no understanding of habit and no memory of having violated my pledge, I said yes. That's where the memory burns brightest: the presentation of the wool sleeve to my eyes, the sighting of the evidence, and the ensuing pulling of the rest of my body into the house, where I was sent to my room.

The second memory is more embarrassing because I was older, about eleven. Like most boys of that age, we sought pictures of women, women who were scantily dressed. Because I had an aunt who subscribed to *Vogue*, which one of the boys told me was a dirty magazine, I was sent to clip pictures from it. Because she lived downstairs from us and worked as a secretary during the day, it was easy to do. I simply attacked her magazine rack with a pair of scissors, clipping all the underwear ads I could find. The boys were satisfied and divided them up, and I, too, filled my pockets. The next day, my mother put a crumpled pile of clippings on my dresser and asked where I got them. I lied. I said Charlie gave them to me. I was embarrassed twice, first for my cutting up my aunt's magazine, and second, for the ridiculous way I had done the job. The women were cut out in silhouettes, and in the perfectly modest advertisements of the fifties, they seemed silly to me even then. My mother was satisfied with my lie and I ran out of the house as fast I could, to escape my mother's face, my lie, and myself. But just as I zoomed down the stairs, I saw my aunt standing in her living room, holding her magazine with the most puzzled expression on her face. Lacy snippets of pages hung from the thick body of the magazine—how could I have forgotten that the ragged *Vogue* would surely be unearthed? That evening, as I ran up the stairs as fast I had run down, she opened her door.

"John," she said very softly, "please leave my magazines alone."

"Okay," I said, and raced onward, slipping along the worn carpet and scrambling on my knees for a step or two.

OVER THE YEARS, I've remained fascinated by the turning up of evidence in every day life. But when I was called for jury duty, I had the chance to see official evidence revealed. It was a civil suit and the plaintiff, Mr. Wilks, complained that he had lost the strength in his hands as a result of his car accident with the defendant. He claimed that he lost his job and could no longer play baseball, which he loved, because he couldn't hold a bat. Although I couldn't discuss it with them, I felt that my fellow jury members were sympathetic.

But then came the evidence. The defendant had hired a friend to follow Mr. Wilks around and videotape his day-to-day activities. The film was shown to all of us, including Mr. Wilks. The film showed him at a job lifting six-foot-long rolls of carpeting onto his shoulders and loading them into a truck. The film went on for some time, and Mr. Wilks did the job well. The next segment showed him shooting basketballs from the half-court line at a local schoolyard.

Needless to say, Mr. Wilks did not collect on his case. And I imagine that when that VCR was rolled out in the court, for everyone to see, and as the tape began to roll, Mr. Wilks must have felt as I did when that sleeve was held up to my eyes.

Evidence is hard to avoid, and people will go to great lengths to dispose of it. I read that in Nigeria two men were arrested for walking down the streets of the major city of Lagos carrying stolen radios and televisions. They were shocked when they were arrested. Why? Because they had just come from a witch doctor whom they had paid to grant them the power to make stolen goods invisible!

Imagine them leaving the witch doctor's house, giggling over their new plans, and then breaking into the first appliance store they see, blithely carrying out stereos and televisions. And think of the life they dreamed of: every day choosing new items from shops and warehouses. Then think of their shock when the police walked right up to them, and a crowd gathered, everyone standing around in the open air and staring at the objects of their desires, which they had tried so desperately to keep hidden.

A Different
Point of View

MY COUSIN DIANE worked as a real estate agent in Connecticut and sold big houses, huge places that most of us will never see the insides of, much less live in. During one of my visits, she invited me to come along while she showed a house to an interested couple. I went out of curiosity, but what I learned there, by overhearing the words of an older man, a painter, who owned the house, I have never forgotten.

The prospective buyers were wealthy businesspeople in their fifties, looking for a place close to New York, but still in the country. We drove there in Diane's company car, a comfortable Chrysler New Yorker, as she pointed out the other estates, the country club, the easiest ways to the highway. They were pleasant people and they enjoyed hearing stories about the person who currently owned the home, the painter. He had an international reputation and was moving to Long Island where his daughter lived. Although his fortune was secure, he held classes in his home for aspiring artists, just for the pleasure of it.

A housekeeper let us in and said that a class had just ended, and although the artist was still addressing the students in an informal way in the living room, we shouldn't worry about disrupting them.

It was a grand Tudor house with an endless driveway. The large rooms were filled with antiques and heavy, carved furniture that fit comfortably under the tall ceilings. Diane showed the buyers room after room, view upon view, and I could tell they liked it.

My job was to open each door and let everyone in as Diane described what we were seeing. Everything went along fine until I opened the basement door. Then I saw something I would never have expected in a house of this kind. Standing at the top of the stairs and sniffing his big nose, was a rat weighing about two pounds. Diane, always first to enter, glanced down quickly and while I stood dumbstruck, she said brightly, "Mustn't let kitty out!" and she closed the door.

Diane has a quick wit, but she is also an honest person, and later in the day she ordered an exterminator to rid the mansion of its pests from top to bottom.

As my cousin and the couple talked in the kitchen, I listened to the artist answer the questions of his students, who were mostly in their forties and fifties.

One student talked about a problem. He said, "When I go to paint a still life, I arrange the flowers in a vase on the table. I take such care when I arrange them, that by the time I get back behind my easel to paint them, they look posed, too posed, and they lose all their freshness."

The artist thought for a minute. Then he said, "After you arrange the flowers the way you usually do, walk around and paint them from the other side of the table."

DIANE DID SELL the house to that couple, and she later told me how thrilled they were with it. And for several weeks, I kept thinking about the place, especially about the artist's words to that student. He was advising the student to look at things from another angle, an easy thing to do, and yet not often done. We rest easy in the familiar.

When I was cutting the lawn the other night, I got the idea to apply the teacher's words. When the mower ran out of gas, instead of rushing to fill the tank, I stopped and walked over to my house. I looked in the windows instead of looking out of them. I had never realized how many toys lay on the dining room table and were stuffed into the shelves of the bookcase; that there were so many photographs of places and people on the walls; and how the three bird cages really took over the living room. It was like looking at a stranger's place and it told me things about myself and my family: what we love, our priorities, who is important to us.

Sometimes you have to take the opposite point of view to see what's really going on around you, to look inward instead of looking out.

I often think of that art student, after his teacher spoke to him. I see him moving his easel to the other side of the table, and struggling with the temptation to change what is not quite right, and then realizing that the fading blossom, the wayward browning leaves and spidery stems, are not what spoil the arrangement, but what make the picture true, and with this realization, his canvas begins to come to life.

Thou Shalt Not

WE TELL CHILDREN what not to do just after they've done it. But worse is telling both children and adults what not to do before they've even thought of it.

I once saw a sign at a small midwestern zoo. It was in front of a coyote cage, which was placed away from the rest of the park, set into the side of a hill. The hill was for the visitors to climb and feel they were among wildlife. The coyotes had no way of knowing where they were at all, since the cage was a confining rectangle, and the walls were cinderblock. The sign I'm talking about said, DO NOT HOWL AT THE COYOTES. Howling at the coyotes was not the first thing that occurred to me as I stood in front of these wretched half-lidded, scraggly beasts who lay on the rough concrete near a trickle of water that filled a small pool in the corner of the cage. In fact, howling at the coyotes was not something that occurred to me at all. Until I read the sign. Then I immediately wondered what would happen if I let up a howl. There was no one around. I faced the coyotes alone on that hill. After a few moments, I resisted the temptation and moved on.

The next amusement was a little playground over the

other side of the slope where kids were swinging and sliding. As I stood watching them I heard a howl, a human howl like the one I suppressed. Then followed a terrific animal howl, the call of the coyote. This went on for the rest of the hour that I walked around that zoo. Even as I left the gates, I heard more howling, human voices desperately trying to imitate the coyote, to see what would happen.

That sign was their inspiration.

I saw a similar sign in an enormous pet store and aquarium in New York. On Church Street, this place was a block long, filled with all kinds of tropical fish for the hobbyist. Aside from the wide collection of fish, they sold bizarre accessories: coffee tables made of glass tanks and pairs of shoes with transparent high heels that could contain water and a fish.

I stopped by every time I was in the neighborhood, marveling at the blind cave fish. Their eyes were covered by scales because they had evolved in the depths of a cave where there was no light at all. A sign said they would bump into the objects in a tank only once, and then memorize them, and swim clearly around the tank from then on. Better than most with eyes!

But it was the octopus I loved best. I am always surprised when I see an octopus in a tank. I think of them as big as a man, probably from all the cartoons I watched as a kid, when their arms swoop after divers. This octopus was about eight inches high, and housed in a tank which didn't give him much room to move. He usually stayed stuck to the front glass, looking out. He had tiny eyes that were full of expression. I used to say a few words to him and then move on.

One day, when I stopped in after being away for a few months, I noticed a new sign on the tank: DO NOT WAVE AT OCTOPUS. Needless to say, this sign floored me. In all the time I had visited the octopus, I had never once thought to wave. Now I wanted to pass my hand before him, gently, to see how he would respond. Again, I resisted and the poor guy clung to his corner, just waiting for someone to take up the question of what would happen if they waved.

How many times have you seen someone observing a display in a store, perhaps an electric train setup, or a nativity scene in a department store? Inevitably, the sign above a particularly beautiful and delicate component reads, DO NOT TOUCH, and so you are all the more drawn to it. I like watching people approach these things, people of all ages, old ladies, young fathers, you see them look at the display, their eyes glowing, and then they light up even more. They have spotted the irresistible, and then above it, the sign: DO NOT TOUCH. At this they consider the object further, then they slowly turn, just a movement of the neck, as they crane left and right to see if anyone will notice as they reach. . . .

I doubt they would have been tempted if not for the sign.

But we have been brought up like this. The Ten Commandments are mostly negative. If "Love Thy Neighbor as Thyself" were followed, then you wouldn't kill, covet, or steal, but the commandment not to do something inspires the meditation of the act, if not the act itself.

I was in a restaurant the other day, and printed on the cocktail napkin was the message: DO NOT OPEN. Inside was a menu of appetizers. (Of course, I couldn't resist.) A good stunt playing on this idea, but I wasn't in the mood for buffalo wings.

Once in Jackson Heights, I saw a man sitting behind a card table which he had set up on the sidewalk. He had a pile of papers in front of him, and urged passersby to sign a petition. I stopped and asked what it was for. He told me it was a petition to remove a billboard set high on the outside of the elevated train station. I hadn't ever noticed it, but he pointed it out: a woman in a bathing suit, a skimpy bikini, advertising something which I forget. It was a big sign, but it was placed so high that none of us walking toward the train ever saw it. It's better to watch where you're going than where this man's mind had led him. He was so shaken that he tried to shake us up as well, and I have to admit, I did look at it from then on.

Another time, in Penn Station, a woman had her table set up with a computer on it. She wanted to show everyone some terrible computer games. She was right; the ones she showed were terrible. The object of one was to attack an Indian tied to a post—but how many of us would have seen such a game if not for her? Meanwhile, wiseguys crowded around her, asking where they could get copies.

An Amateur's
Guide to Fishing

IT'S PRIME FISHING TIME, and I'm the newcomer to a small town on Cape Cod, where I'm also the butt of good-natured jokes by the locals because of all the fishing lore I pry from them at little league games, barbecues, and other events.

A year after we moved here, my ten-year-old son asked for a fishing rod for his birthday. I had fished only a few times in my life, as a kid, when my father took me out of Queens to Freeport, Long Island, or to Sheepshead Bay in Brooklyn. We planned this for months, and got up before dawn to drive out to the party boats. Here on the Cape, living a mile from the bay and even less from the ocean, it's something that boys do twice a day without thinking.

A few months ago, I went to Kmart and bought two rods and reels, a tackle box, lures, everything the salesman said we needed to cast from the shore. At the beach, an old-timer showed me how to tie the line to a swivel and how to fling it into the ocean. A week later, my son reeled in a thirty-inch bluefish. Once it was on the shore, he turned his attention to me. Ten is a funny age, a pendulum swinging between childhood and adolescence. In the joy of his success and in the weary aftermath of his struggle with the big fish, he yelled, "Dad, kiss me!" and then as a second thought, he held up his palm for a high five.

The more we learned from our friends, the more we visited tackle shops, buying our share of wily lures. It was the start of an addiction, an amateur's passion. And it was also the beginning of odd fantasies, born from standing for hours on an empty beach and staring at the horizon. Sometimes I felt like we were flirting. If a rig didn't work after fifteen minutes, we'd switch to a brighter lure, perhaps one with red eyes and a fluorescent tail. Other times, I dreamed we were taking a chance on the lottery—looking over the endless ocean, what were the chances that a striped bass would pass before our lines and choose our twirling ounce of metal?

Sometimes, when we caught a slew of fish, some of them undersized, I had a strangely omnipotent feeling, as if I were St. Peter at the pearly gates; a few would be saved, others doomed. Looking into the glaring eyes of a caught fish, and trying to unhook him gently, to throw him back unhurt, I felt merciful. I was also glad that the fish couldn't understand me when I reeled in a small bass, his gills and mouth gruesomely snared by a long lure. At those times I'd yell out, upon his arrival at my feet, "Oh no! Look at this one!" I imagined standing at heaven's gate and being greeted by those woeful words!

My son and I got better at the sport, learning things we never dreamed of: that hooks have to be sharpened, that you have to gauge the direction of the wind. But along the way we had our share of humiliations.

One day, arriving at the beach in the early morning, we set up right in front of the parking lot, something we never did, as the beach crowd takes over this area when the sun is high. But since it was early, we fished there. In the timelessness of casting into the rising and falling waves, we hadn't noticed that the beach filled up behind us. It was still too chilly for swimming, so the beach goers just sat there staring out.

It was then that I learned another lesson: there was sea-weed in the water and it kept getting lumped on my lure. With each retrieve, I had to pick it off, but not knowing yet how to do it easily, I kept stretching up to the tip of my nine-foot rod to grasp the hook. It swung back and forth as I groped toward it, and one time it flew past my fingers, right at me, taking the baseball cap off my head and dangling it back and forth as I lunged after it. When I turned around, I saw I was on stage and fifty or more people had their eyes on what looked like a scene from a Jerry Lewis movie.

We've gotten better at it now, still learning, but at least no longer falling off the two-foot underwater ledge that forms our favorite beach, the Head of the Meadow, something I did once on a particularly vigorous cast. And we enjoy our talks with the natives. Last week, an old fisherman asked my son if he liked fishing, to which my son replied he did. "Good," the old man said, "because you can't get into any trouble when you're fishing." And when I remarked how much time we'd been spending at the beach, he said, "That doesn't matter. Time spent fishing doesn't count toward your life span, it's extra."

Still, when I cast, I'm all elbows and effort, the trans-planted New Yorker getting used to the sand in his shoes. My son, on the other hand, whips his rod far into the surf with the grace of one who learns early. He's the kid I used to see at the shore when I was a kid from the city, the one my father used to ask for directions and who told us which fish were running, what fun it was, and how to get there.

Directions that have taken me forty years to follow.

Suspicion

ONCE I WAS SUSPECTED of a crime. I was living in a very small town in a furnished room above my landlady. Across the hall from me lived a quiet couple. The landlady and her husband had a seven-year-old boy, Philip, with whom I often played catch. It was a peaceful house, except for when the couple across the way had a few glasses of wine at night and then they strummed a guitar and played calypso music. I can never hear those songs about loading the banana boats without thinking of my neighbors' spirited singing and the pleasure it gave them.

As my friend says, "There's something for everybody."

One night there was a knock at my door. When I opened it, a small, heavyset man who identified himself as a detective looked me in the eye and held out his badge. He held the badge low and off to the side, so that I had to make an effort to see it. At the same time, I felt him watching my face, to see, perhaps, if my expression was one of guilt. It was a neat ploy and I admired it.

He explained that the apartment across the way had been robbed and asked if I knew anything about it. I said that

I did not, and he asked if I had heard anything strange, which I hadn't.

As we began to chat, I guess he released me from suspicion because he seemed more relaxed.

"I think it was a female," he said, putting his hands into his pockets, "because some jewelry had been dumped into the fish tank and swirled around. You know, they played around in there."

Why jewelry swirled around a fish tank would point to a female I could not fathom, but these are the ways of a small-town detective.

The next day, the landlady stopped me on the way out. We had always been friendly, but this time I felt she looked at me a little differently.

"I understand you spoke with Detective Fryer," she said.

I explained that I hadn't heard anyone prowling around next door, although I never really listened very hard. She just nodded.

These kind of things make me feel like confessing immediately, and saying, "Yes, I did it!"

But I just said something like I hoped he'd get to the bottom of it.

I never heard from the detective again and eventually I forgot about the whole thing. A couple of months later the landlady stopped me as I was going up the steps.

"I have something to tell you," she said sheepishly. "We found the rest of the jewelry."

"Where?" I asked.

Blushing, she said, "It was in my husband's briefcase and

stuck under our bed. We think Philip just got into some mischief and hid it there."

"Oh," I said. "Kids do stuff like that sometimes."

"I'm sorry for any trouble it caused," she said.

"No trouble," I said.

I pictured the impish Philip swirling the pearls and rhinestones in among the angel fish. So it wasn't a female after all.

That night my neighbors sang "Day-O" as usual, and I had to laugh when I thought about the landlady opening her husband's attaché case.

There is something for everyone.

There's calypso music for some, the thrill of swirling jewels for another, the satisfaction of cooking up a theory for someone else, and for me, the memory of an old saying: Because we are human, nothing is alien to us.

The Lost Son

THE SUMMER I WAS FIFTEEN I worked as a messenger at Paramount Pictures. My Aunt Linda worked there and got me a job in the mailroom, for which I was grateful.

On one of my first days there, when we left together for lunch, she stopped suddenly in the lobby, in front of an older man in a uniform, the elevator starter. Those were the days when there were still elevator operators, and they flung the beautifully polished brass gates back and forth across the car's entrance with a flourish. The starter's job was to make sure that the cars were servicing all the floors in the twenty-seven story building, and that the men were given appropriate breaks from the schedule.

The first words my aunt spoke to the starter were, "Bert, when did your son die?"

"December 11, 1949," he said.

"This is my nephew John," she said, and I shook his hand. "That's the day he was born," she continued, pointing to me.

I was stunned. With no warning of what this conversation was to be about, and prepared only for small pleasantries, I was suddenly facing a long-bereaved man to whose grief I was co-incidentally linked.

"My whole life stopped the day he died," he said. "I wish it had been me."

"I'm sorry," I said.

"Every year I write a poem to him," he said.

"He puts it in the *Daily News*," my aunt said.

"I publish it on December 11. Every year. I don't show it to my wife until it comes out."

I looked back and forth from the starter to my aunt. They were both looking at me. For the rest of the summer, as I walked past the podium which Bert peered over in the marble lobby, and he nodded at me, I felt like a ghost, a person who had somehow been given life by his son's death.

Since that time, I have met men whose work has stopped because of a death. Dodge MacKnight, the great American watercolorist, never picked up a brush after his son's death in the Spanish-American War. I spoke with a novelist recently who said he hasn't written a word since the death of his brother.

Bert was the first man I met who began to write due to a loss, an evolving epitaph, comforting to him and his wife.

Good Intentions

HOW MANY TIMES have good intentions gone bad? Several times for me. When I first moved into an apartment building, I was anxious to meet as many tenants as I could. One morning, when the elevator arrived on the fifth floor where I lived, an elderly lady stood there and asked if this were her floor. "Five?" she said.

"Yes," I answered, and I stepped forward to help her with her load. She stood behind a chair on casters, a chair piled high with clean, folded laundry. When I rolled the chair out of the elevator for her and onto the fifth floor landing, she called, "No, no!" Looking back inside, I saw her clinging to the walls of the elevator—I had removed not the burden I thought to lighten, but her walker, which doubled as her laundry cart. I spent the next weeks apologizing.

IN A COLLEGE in upstate New York, another case of good intentions gone bad occurred. It was a hilly town, and some fraternity boys made use of the landscape in the winter by sledding down a steep hill on the main street of the campus. When a boy's sled flipped over the curb, he hit his head and died. The campus community wanted to memorialize him. The fraternity brothers chipped in and had a six-foot stone monument erected on the spot, with a brass plaque dedicated to the student's memory and his membership in their club.

But the next year, another boy went down the same hill, crashed into the monument and he died too, like lightning striking twice.

I MADE A FUNNY MISTAKE ONCE, at Wake Forest University, where I was giving a talk. The lecture was supposed to take place on the beautiful porch of the Reynolda House, which overlooked green and rolling acres. After I was introduced, music from a live band from a fraternity party began to blare. I couldn't talk over "Born to Be Wild," so they moved the lecture to a library, but the woman directing the lecture series worried that I would be interrupted by some people coming late, because she left a sign on the outdoor podium stating that the location had been changed.

She was right. For the first few minutes, people poked their heads into the library, as if to ask, "Is this is the place?" and I would signal them to enter, which they did.

About twenty minutes later, a couple stood in the hall, and then peeked in, curious. I signaled them and they jumped back, embarrassed. I signaled them again, heartily, but they waved their hands as if to say, "No!"

Still, they lingered. Finally, I stopped and addressed them directly. "Come on in," I said. "Interruptions don't bother me."

They looked at each other and then sat down quickly. Satisfied with my generosity and unflappability, I continued to talk.

When the lecture was over, and we walked out of the room, I was chagrined to notice that right next to the entrance to the library was an elevator. That couple I thought terribly late had only been waiting for an elevator and I had obviously dragged them into my lecture.

Sometimes we try so hard to be liked or to be remembered that we get wrapped up in our own worlds, and when we look out of them, we can't see straight.

The Problem Solver

ANNE STEVENS, the dean at the small college where I worked, was a woman of many abilities, among them her knack for solving problems in the most unconventional way.

There was a dangerous road that cut right through the campus, used heavily by tractor-trailers and hot rodders. The college president wrote letters to the governor to get it rerouted, and when that request was denied, we asked for a blinking light, which was also denied. A little campus did not merit much attention from the state house, and so Anne suggested a solution that at first seemed like a joke, but it worked.

"Let's get the woodworking crew to make a sign, a sign that looks like those the Department of Transportation puts up. It will be big and yellow, with black letters, and in the shape of a diamond. It will say one word: BUMP."

The carpentry crew made the perfect sign, and when it was posted, cars zooming through the campus slowed down to a crawl, their drivers leaning over the dashboards, peering toward the road. It worked for years, and I bet it's still there today.

When we walked out of that meeting about the road, I

kidded her about her idea, and she mentioned a professional problem solver she had read about. He was used mainly by cities and companies who couldn't afford conventional solutions.

Back in her office, she made two cups of tea and lit a cigarette.

"One city called him because they were having a problem with cars parking downtown all day long. They couldn't afford parking meters. His solution was to pass a law that said when you parked downtown you had to leave your headlights on. So they hired a few people to give tickets to those with no lights on. The others moved fast."

She gave me another example. The owner of an old office building was getting complaints from his tenants because the elevators were too slow and they had to wait too long. The building had ten floors and the owner couldn't afford to upgrade the elevators or add another one. The solution was to install full-length mirrors on the wall between the elevators on each floor. Soon, the complaints stopped. People were so busy looking at their reflections that the time passed quickly, and they didn't notice the wait.

Anne was full of such stories, and had mastered the thinking behind them, perfect for a college on a small budget, as well as for the world.

Time

SOMEONE ONCE SAID that each man's philosophy is like the time on his watch. Each is different, but each thinks his own is right.

When my friend Michael visited New York for the day, we had a great time. We went to the Museum of Modern Art and to Ripley's Believe It or Not Museum. At the Modern Art, there was a machine that spat silver dollars and destroyed itself. In Ripley's there was a different machine, a kind of wagon wheel with steel balls in it. Each time a ball dropped, the wheel turned an inch and another ball dropped. The sign next to it said PERPETUAL MOTION MACHINE.

When evening came, I was due in Queens, at my mother's apartment for dinner. Michael had other friends to meet at six o'clock.

We sat on benches in a tiny park in Greenwich Village. It was a lovely autumn evening, and the shadows were just beginning to surround the fruit store's crates of oranges and lemons, and to creep around the doorways of those great Italian restaurants. Michael asked me for the time, and I said, 5:15. We were on schedule and continued to talk. He asked me a little later and I said 5:15 again. Neither of us noticed. We were still going on and enjoying each other's company. About a half hour went by and I answered once more: 5:15.

"You said that before," he said.

"What?" I asked. "This watch is always right."

"No," he said. "Let's check." A passerby told us it was 6:00. We were both late and I dashed into the subway and he raced uptown.

On the train, a friendly disagreement started between a couple. The man said it was 6:10 and the woman said it was 6:00. Our car was crowded and many hands clung to the same pole, like spokes off an axle. The couple decided to ask the man next to me, whose watch showed on his wrist. He said it was 6:10. The first man said to his partner, "I told you so."

Not satisfied, she turned to me.

"Excuse me," she said. "What time do you have?"

I couldn't explain that my watch had just stopped less than an hour before. It seemed too absurd. Instead, I just rolled up my sleeve, glanced down, and held it out for her to read.

"I have 5:15," I said. And as New Yorkers have learned to do, she kept her surprise to herself and changed the conversation with her partner, afraid of further disturbing a nut in his own little world.

I was late for dinner, but what better excuse than, "My watch stopped," with the watch's frozen face to prove it. And although I was in my thirties, I still liked to have good excuses for my mother.

The World Authority on Silkworms

IN COLLEGE I took a general science course with a professor named Frank Musa. Frank was a likable fellow, and I was surprised at how well he knew the varied fields we studied. But biology was his specialty. He would often stop a student in the middle of a report and comment how he personally knew the scientist being cited, and then he'd tell an anecdote about him or her. It seemed he knew everybody, and after a while I wondered whether he made a lot of this up.

During one of our seminar discussions about the mating habits of different species, Musa went off on a tangent about a silkworm farm that he had researched up in Amherst, Massachusetts, and the reasons for its failure.

He spoke in the same way he always did, but I never forgot this peculiar digression. He said, "The silkworm really hasn't been examined fully as to why it sometimes conceives and sometimes fails to conceive. I'm working on a project that will unravel its patterns. Soon I'll be known as the world's expert in infertility in the silkworm." As he said this with a smile, the remarks passed, but his strange claim stayed with me.

I became friendly with Frank and he sometimes came to my dormitory for a beer, a place no other professor would be seen.

Years after I left college, I was reading *The New York Times* one day and there was a headline about Musa making the breakthrough he had boasted about. The story of that silkworm farm and his findings were being published by a big press in New York.

At that point I began to evaluate all the things Frank had said, and which I had dismissed. I guess he *had* known all those scientists.

I saw him years later in a French restaurant in New York, an inexpensive place named Larre's. It was the opening night of a big retrospective at the Whitney Museum of the paintings of Myron Stout. Myron was in his seventies and getting national recognition. I had invited my parents because they had never been to an event like this. Because I knew Myron, I had a pocketful of invitations to the reception.

Frank was with a group of men, all professors, tweedy and distinguished looking. He was interested in the celebration at the museum, and I gave him a stack of passes.

It was a great night for Myron. Reviewers from the major papers and art journals surrounded him and his work. I recall that my mother, however, did not appreciate the minimalist abstract black-and-white paintings, and commented that they looked like the x-rays of teeth.

In the crush of the crowd, I felt a tap on my shoulder and there was Frank, this time surrounded by women he had brought in with him and who seemed to be acquaintances made very recently, like in the past few hours. One had a French accent, and responded to whatever he said, with the words, "Oh, Frank!"

I WENT BACK to my alma mater years later, to give a talk, which was scheduled on April Fool's Day, a fitting day for an alum's return. Frank was not there anymore. The other department members said he had suffered a breakdown, and no one knew where he was.

Then one night in Grand Central Station, I sat on a bench waiting for a train. It was after midnight, and the homeless were wandering in for warmth.

On the bench behind me, I heard the drunken boasts of a man saying he was once a star hockey player. "I was so famous," he said, "I would only play home games, never traveled."

Then another voice broke in, this one with an accent. "I had two cars, a Cadillac and a Lincoln. Now what do I have? Two legs to walk!"

After more discussion, a third voice said, "I was in the *New York Times*. No one knows more about silkworms than I do."

I was sure I had misunderstood. I was not listening very carefully, but I leaned around and saw my old teacher.

He was in a good overcoat that had not been kept well, and his eyes, which always had a sagging, triangular shape, seemed even more forlorn.

I stood near him and said, "Frank?"

"Nah," he said, and got up, moving away from me. I followed him.

"Frank," I said, identifying myself.

"I'm not Frank," he said, "but I could use some help."

I paused. I wanted to give him more than money and as I tried to figure out what I could do, he misinterpreted my hesitation for refusal.

"Look," he said, as he shifted restlessly. "Are you gonna help me out or not?"

"Yes," I said, and gave him some bills which he took, and then nodded and rushed off.

At home, I dug up my copy of his book and looked at his photo on the back.

The train station seems an eerie and awful place to say good-bye to someone for the last time. Frank was an important teacher to me and more than that, a man. He made me listen to all men a little harder, be a little less skeptical, and I think of him often.

Wishes

WHEN CERTAIN PEOPLE want something, they'll wish for something else. The other day, one of my friends said, "I wish Holly's husband would get a job on the West Coast so they'll move. Then when her job opens up in the office, I'll be the one to get it."

"That's a long way of wishing for money," I said. "Why not just wish for the dough?"

"This wish is more possible," she said, laughing.

"But since we're wishing," I said, "don't wish for a roundabout way of getting it."

Wishes should be direct. My friend wanted money and invented a way to get it that made her feel better than the bluntness of her wish. It made her goal seem more realistic, but it was just as dreamy.

A FRIEND TOLD ME a fable about a man who quit his job so he could find the formula for making gold. He worked for ten years, and made progress, but he got stuck at a certain point in the process. He tried over and over again, but he continued to be stymied at the same stage.

He heard about a very wise woman who lived in Africa. She was said to have worked through this formula and seemed to be the one to answer his questions. She was a wise woman who knew secrets of all kinds, but she lived quietly in a hut with her family and did not exploit her knowledge.

The man searched for her. He spent another ten years tracking her down, and he finally found the village near her dwelling. The night before he visited her he couldn't sleep, he was so excited about solving the difficult formula and discovering the way to make gold so he'd be rich. He lay in bed thinking, "I've spent twenty years of my life for this moment, and tomorrow I'll have the answer. I'll go home, make gold, and have my fortune."

The next day he walked the long road to her house. He arrived at noon and knocked on the door. A beautiful woman answered, the most beautiful woman he had ever seen, and he was struck breathless. He asked for the wise woman, and the woman at the door said it was she. He was thunderstruck again. He had pictured the wise woman as an old hag. Still at the door, he told her what he wanted, that he had taken the formula to a certain stage, and so on. But he still could not take his eyes off her.

She held up her hand and said, "I know the formula you are talking about and I can help you. But because of all the work I have, and the many pilgrims that visit me, I have a rule: I will allow you one question and one question only. It is a hard-and-fast rule. Now hurry, because my husband is away and I have a lot of things to do before he returns."

Heart pounding, and still staring at the beautiful woman, the man couldn't help himself, and asked in a rush, "When is your husband coming back?"

And so the man used up his single question, one that showed that for his whole life he was searching for the wrong thing. He did not want gold, or even riches. He wanted women. He wished for the means to get them, and when he met the wise woman, his true passion was revealed. He forgot his misguided life's work in the flash of seeing his real desire before him.

I HAVE A COUSIN who wanted to make a dashing appearance, so he bought a fancy sports car. What did he really want? Just like the alchemist of the previous story, he wanted women. Salesmen know this weakness of ours: we'll buy an object because we hope it leads to what we really want. When I was a kid my uncle brought me to a prestigious men's clothing store in New York. While he was looking at a shirt, the salesman came up to him and whispered, "One of the Rockefellers was in here just an hour ago, I'm not allowed to tell you which one, but he bought a dozen of that exact shirt." My uncle laughed, just as I did a few years ago in F.A.O. Schwartz, the big toy store, when I idly picked up a cute stuffed animal and the salesperson ran over to me and said, "Mia Farrow bought that same porcupine last week." This must be an old game, to suggest that we can fulfill our wish to be like the rich and celebrated simply by carrying around something like theirs.

There's a character in a novel by Thomas Hardy whom I have never forgotten. He's a police chief who searches for a long time for a man, and he finds him. But this man proves innocent. When asked if he found the man, he answers, "He's the man we were in search of, that's true, and yet he is not the man we were in search of. For the man we were in search of was not the man we wanted."

I wonder how often that is true for all of us, that the object of our search is not really our heart's desire.

Bus Trip

MY AUNT LINDA took me on a bus trip to Williamsburg, Virginia, when I was twelve years old. It was sponsored by Cassar tours, and a master of ceremonies rode in the front of the bus and told stories and jokes, held drawing contests, and entertained us all the way from New York City.

The MC, Steve, held a microphone deftly and put us through routines he must have done hundreds of times. Among the activities was a competition to sketch a cow. In another, we had to guess what vegetable he was thinking of. The prizes, too, were jokes: the promised cigarette lighter turned out to be a book of matches. Another prize, billed as a machine that would x-ray a finger, was a simple cardboard tube with a feather pasted at the far end. To a twelve year old, these were funny, even if they were corny.

Steve had a way of asking if we wanted to stop to go to the bathroom; obviously, this bus was not well-equipped. When we'd pass an exit on the highway containing a rest stop, he'd say, "Oui?" and if someone on the bus had to go, they were to yell back, "Oui-oui," which of course also sounded like "wee-wee." See what I mean by corny?

Now that I think of it, I won the poetry contest on the
bus. We had to write a rhyme that used our name as well as
our seat number.

I wrote:

My name is John
I sit in seat Three
You know what I mean
When I say, "Oui, oui."

Second prize went to a cranky old woman named Augusta who
complained about everything, but with a wonderful wit. It was
July and the driver kept the temperature of the bus so low that
Augusta growled constantly about the cold. Her poem went:

I sit in seat Four
My name is Augusta
Turn off the air-conditioning
Before I bust ya

I still think she should have won.

My aunt brought her camera and took pictures of us all
over Williamsburg in the classic tourist poses: our heads and
wrists in the pillory, sitting in the stocks, against fountains and
on lawns full of flowers.

We ate our meals with other people on the bus, in diners
and sometimes in hotels. They were not fancy, but they were
decent, and the Southern menus were interesting. We had pea-

nut soup, chicken-fried steak, and grits with eggs. It was a good experience for a boy from New York.

A woman at our table prayed each night over her food. Each prayer began, "O God, you are my silent partner." I thought it was an engaging way to think of God, as a partner whom you could trust and talk things over with, but my aunt thought differently.

When we were back in our room, she said, "Imagine thinking of yourself as an equal with God!"

I guess you could divide the world of believers into those two camps: those who want a god who is close, a trusted partner, and those who want a god on high, who will look upon us and have mercy.

I saw something else there that was educational: segregated rest rooms. I was amazed the first time I saw the choice of doors: MEN—WHITE and MEN—COLORED. I am always able to retrieve from my memory those doors of such plain and simple wood, adorned with such vicious planks.

I thought of our trip because tonight I found the photos from Williamsburg in a shoebox, along with a trivet I bought for my mother there. It's a wrought iron round thing with General Lee on a horse in its middle. Around it, it says, THE CONFEDERATE STATES OF AMERICA 1861–1865.

Aside from the photos I mentioned, there are a few taken when the bus stopped high on one of the scenic overlooks in the Blue Ridge Mountains. The panoramic views are sweeping and, even in the black-and-white photos, you can still get an idea of the beauty of the place. In one, my aunt stands against a rail with the range behind her, and there's one of me in the same pose. I recall taking one photo in particular. I aimed the camera right above the highest range and shot the sky just for the fun of it. The photo is before me, all sky, few clouds. You could never tell that below it lies the long and breathtaking mountain range, that under it are many commuters, tourists, buses, and a boy and his aunt. That under it there was so much to be learned, not only by a boy, but by men and women. It could have been anywhere, and yet it wasn't: it was 1963, in Virginia, and the earth was spinning under those clouds when the camera stopped it long enough for me to pause over this box of photographs tonight and remember.

The Christmas Tree

MY FIRST YEAR TEACHING at an Ivy League college was an experience different from my other jobs, teaching and otherwise: the students were gifted and many were wealthy. When we read an essay that mentioned a statue in Rome, several had seen the statue as children. One student had a chauffeur and limousine waiting outside the classroom, and I sometimes thought I could hear the motor running as I talked. Such wealth had its privileges and its drawbacks.

During my first year there, the president gave a Christmas party for the faculty. The president's house was a Tudor mansion, with little towers peaking from its orange-tiled roof and big windows crisscrossed with lead. I had heard this was an event not to be missed, and faculty cars lined the circular drive.

The inside of the mansion glowed with Christmas cheer. Lights were strung from the ceiling and holly and wreaths of all kinds graced the doors. Goblets of shrimp were placed around the rooms, along with platters of cold meats and cheese. Bowls of punch and bottles of wine glowed along a sideboard. Now I knew why my colleagues told me to be sure to attend. Usually the lunches in the faculty dining room consisted of what the students were served for dinner the night before. Because I was new, I introduced myself to those around me.

Each person I met had accomplished a great deal. A woman in the art history department was writing a biography of Matisse. A video artist had just made a series of photographs that were hung in a subway tunnel so that the passengers looking out the windows would in effect be seeing a movie as they rode.

However, after biographies were exchanged, conversation fell flat, and people went from room to room, looking at the paintings on the walls, the design of the great rooms, and each other.

In the main room, the center of which was a blazing fireplace, I saw something I had never seen before: a Christmas tree about eight feet tall and along each branch, little candles blazed from their foil holders. It was beautiful and I stopped to admire it.

In this room too, the talk was hushed, as if in a library. The festive decorations, the generous and even extravagant food, made an odd contradiction to the very formal manner of those attending. All talk started and stopped, leaving big holes in the atmosphere.

I remembered reading that when the director of a play needed crowd noise for a scene, he commanded half the cast to yell, "Rhubarb, rhubarb," and the other half to whisper, "Vichyssoise, vichyssoise." If that director had been at this party, he might have ordered it.

A few of us were talking in front of the tree, searching for things to say, when I noticed a man sitting next to it, with no drink, no napkin wrapped around a chicken wing. I introduced myself.

Embarrassed, he stayed seated.

"Oh," he said, "you don't have to meet me. I'm just here to make sure the tree doesn't catch fire." He lifted up the fire extinguisher by his side, which he had kept hidden.

"What kind of tree is this?" one of the faculty asked, and the man rose and told her. Another asked how the candles were fastened, and the tree's guardian explained how he put it together. Suddenly the tree was surrounded by people, all admiring and asking questions, not of each other's accomplishments, but of things outside themselves, and about how one of the world's trees wound up in this room, dressed and hung with fire. The room began buzzing, and the shy man answered all the questions put to him, and soon he held a glass of punch as well.

I drove home thinking that the party came to life when people stopped worrying about who they were, where they were, and how they were supposed to act. The presence of a simple tree changed all that and set us free.

Ritual at
A Pizza Parlor

I MENTIONED EARLIER that I had a scare with a brain tumor a few years back. While I was recovering from surgery, I established some important rituals. One involved a restaurant named Frank's Roman Pizza.

My son was five when I went through this ordeal. I was still feeling the full effects of having a quarter-sized hole drilled into the back of my head, and he used to stand by my chair with an airplane made out of balsa wood. Before the operation, we played a lot together, and it would be a while before I got back into the swing of things. Some days my headaches were severe, but even then I did not realize how much I had changed in the eyes of my son. At those times, he'd ask, full of concern, "Are you going to talk in your low voice today?"

After a few weeks, I felt well enough to drive, but if I turned too quickly to the left or right, I got dizzy. This was one of the effects of the operation: I was off balance.

My son loved pizza, so the first place we went was Frank's. Frank was a hairy guy with a big mustache. There's a rough statue of him in the restaurant, cut out of wood by an artist who used a chainsaw. It's a dark place, with booths stained deep brown, and walls covered with the framed sketches customers drew on napkins. Let's put it this way: it's a dump, but I love it.

We ordered our slices, played a game of pinball, and then I put a quarter into the jukebox: "If I Were A Rich Man," by Zero Mostel, and "Mama" by Jimmy Roselli. The Mostel song went on forever, and I bet nobody who heard it could get it out of their heads for the rest of the day. Roselli is one of those Italian singers whose voice shakes with melodrama and I was in the mood for that as I watched the other customers come in and order against the background of napkins.

Those first days I was back on my feet were precious to me. Even now, when I go out for pizza with my son, just the two of us, I feel very emotional, no matter where it is: Spiritus Pizza, George's Pizza, or Villa Pizza, to name a few we go to. It's sentimental, I know, to make this connection. But I saw the privilege of driving a few miles and walking through a restaurant's door as just that: a privilege I had been denied for weeks and might have been denied forever.

How tenderly I treated everything in those days, as if everything had just been born.

It reminded me of a time when my mother was in New York Hospital for the removal of a malignant growth. My father and I waited for the results of the operation in the large waiting room which overlooks York Avenue. It's a big, bright room, with glass walls. You can see out to the street below very easily. I watched others leaving the hospital as they flagged cabs. Usually, New Yorkers are quite aggressive hailing a taxi. They cut in front of each other, argue, and sometimes jump into someone else's cab. The people leaving the hospital were the opposite: They were in a rush like the rest, but they were absolutely courteous, even generous to each other. Some might have been patients who were just released, others were visitors to stricken friends or loved ones. All were touched by a common mortality, and when you walk so close to death, you don't push those around you. You see that you are all headed in the same direction.

Even today, when I walk into a pizza parlor, the days of my recuperation rise up before me and I see myself as I was then, just happy to be out and about. Just plain happy. I play an old record and recall the boy by the chair holding the airplane, and I imagine myself taking it into the backyard and throwing it high into the sky, as high as I am able, and then we both watch with delight as we wait for it to sail back down.

The Holy Ghost

BEING RAISED CATHOLIC, I was taught about God, not a singular god, but the Holy Trinity, three persons in one God, the Father, the Son and the Holy Ghost. Our teachers used the three-leaf clover to illustrate the concept: three leaves on the same stem.

The Father was easy to understand. Although the three persons in one were equal, we all felt that the Father was the oldest. The Son, Jesus, was also easy to comprehend: he was a man. The mysterious part of the trinity was the Holy Ghost. As kids we heard of Casper the friendly ghost, and there were scary ghosts, but no holy ghosts. He intrigued us, and the more we read about him, the more interested we became.

WHEN I WAS TEN, my mother lost her voice. She had growths on her vocal cords and, when she spoke, her words came out in a rasp. She had to write everything on a little blackboard, including the simplest directions to me, like, "Brush your teeth." It must have been very hard for her and my father, but I accepted it, as children do, easily and without question.

Her doctors said she would not speak again and, at that

time, she began to pray. A priest told her to make a novena (nine trips to the church in nine weeks) to the Holy Ghost. At the end of the nine weeks, she came home from church and spoke. After going for an entire year without saying a word, her first words were, "Do you want spaghetti tonight?" My father and I spun around in what had been a house of silent rooms. It was not that her voice returned little by little. It returned all at once, full and clear.

After that, my mother continued her prayers to the Holy Ghost, and she kept it up for years. She always wore a medal of the Holy Ghost, a bright bit of red jewelry that didn't look religious unless you inspected it closely. Everywhere I went, I looked in stores for medals and images for her. Even when I was in my twenties, I went to different craft fairs and flea markets, bringing back images of the Holy Ghost, which she wore. This was in the seventies, when the dove was popular as a bird of peace, and these seemed to please her just as well.

I called my mother a few weeks ago, to ask her if she still kept up her devotion to the Holy Ghost.

"I do," she corrected me, "but you know they changed the name to the Holy Spirit now."

It doesn't seem the same, the mystery of the ghost is gone. But if any lesson can be learned from the Holy Ghost, it's that the language doesn't matter. Faith has no language, it's invisible, illogical, and in that we are all joined.

AS I WAS PUTTING these pages into a folder, I noticed on my desk, next to a lump of petrified rock and a plastic armadillo that glows in the dark, a medal that my mother gave me years ago. It is definitely not a simple dove. It's a bird with wings spread powerfully, wearing a tiny, almost invisible crown on its head. On the other side are the words, "Come Holy Ghost Enlighten Me." I've kept it because I'll take any enlightenment offered, no matter where I can get it, from a bird, a spirit, or even a ghost.

Believe Nothing
of What You Hear

MY GRANDMOTHER used to say to me, "Believe nothing of what you hear and only half of what you see." It took me a long time to appreciate her remark, but after years of comic misunderstandings and confusions, I got her point.

Years ago, I worked at a small college in the hills of North Carolina. Half of the campus is set in the middle of a pine forest, and the rest is surrounded by farmland. There are many twists and turns that lead to places like Snake Lake and Vine Holler.

During my first week there, at a gathering of new employees, some of the old-timers spoke to us. We all had to tell a little something about ourselves, and the president introduced the dean by saying he was a scientist who also liked art. He said he was hired "to humanize the sciences and simonize the humanities." It was a friendly, good-hearted affair and, as it was a warm day, we gathered outside the library for a glass of punch and some cookies. The librarian and I hit it off, and she pointed out in the distance a tall mountain and its treeline. She said she'd introduce me to Ellery, who ran the farm, and Susan, who tended the enormous garden. Then she asked, "Have you met Keith, our pastor?"

"Not yet," I said.

"He is always there," she said, "when I get lost along the path."

"What path?" I asked, in an earnest panic.

I asked because I was sure that I, coming from the Northeast, would surely get lost on that path.

Later, back in my cabin, I realized what she meant, and how dumb she must have thought I was.

I could hear my grandmother laughing.

DURING THAT SAME YEAR, I was asked to welcome the students who arrived to begin the January term. We always made sure to greet these new students warmly, because they were often a little skittish. Starting at mid-year was difficult, since everyone else was already familiar with the place. As they pulled up to their dormitories in the school van, I was there to shake their hands and make them feel at home. Vivian, the student I had hired to pick them up at the airport and drive them to campus, was a friendly person, a sociology major, and also a strong woman, because she had to help them load and unload their luggage.

As the new students paraded out of the van, I introduced myself. They walked tilted over, bags and computer boxes weighing them down, tired from the plane ride and the exhaustion that comes from leaving home.

Vivian came up to me and whispered, "People are bringing some heavy baggage with them."

Turning to her, I said, "Well, if it's out of the ordinary, they'll have to carry it themselves."

"No," she said, "some heavy *personal* baggage."

Concerned that she'd be worn out, and wanting to protect the welfare of my worker, I said, "Then just tell them to carry it themselves. Or they can get someone to help them, or they can make two trips."

Lying in bed that night, I finally got it: they had told her some fears and worries and, in my concern about my worker and her load, I hadn't thought about anything else.

Those two things might have gotten me the reputation as a dunce on campus, and among certain groups, I bet they did.

These experiences reminded me of a mistake I made in high school. The three-story school I attended was built like a big horseshoe: one side boys and the other side girls. The top of the horseshoe contained the library, gym, and cafeteria, one on each floor. These were the only places for the genders to interact, and if you wanted to meet a girl, you joined a team, a club, or shuffled through the card catalogue as you glanced around. I joined the yearbook staff because the yearbook committee meetings were held on the girl's side.

The editor, Jean, a lovely and smart girl, asked me one day to help her bring some boxes up from the basement. Once alone in that dark place, I looked around at the stacked chairs, the big artificial Christmas tree, the snow shovels, the cut-outs of leprechauns and derbies dangling over broken parallel bars, and I asked her, "What boxes?" I had to look over her head to say this because she was standing very close to me, her mouth almost touching mine. After a moment in which my eyes searched the room again, she said, "I guess someone must have picked them up already," and we left.

That there were never any boxes occurred to me a year later and I cringed at the recognition. That was an honest innocence, and when I picture myself gazing over Jean's head at the dance decorations, I could give myself a good kick and a bit of advice.

Part of it might be: believe nothing of what you hear, but pay attention to what's going on around you.

Miss Leone

I ADMIT I loved the woman next door, Miss Leone, who lived alone with her white cat, who prepared taffy apples for the kids at Halloween, and who had the craziest theories I've ever heard.

When we moved to this part of town, the neighbors described her in many ways: "a little off"; "not all there"; and "touched." All true, but she was still more wonderful than many of us who are "all there," and she kept life more than interesting. I learned a lot from her.

The first week we lived here, it was autumn, a beautiful morning, and we were each raking leaves in our backyards.

Out of the blue, she said to me, "Last night I flew with the geese." After a few questions, I got her to explain. She said she was out in her yard the night before and a flock of geese flew overhead. For the fun of it, she said, she started flapping her arms along with them and running in their direction.

"The next thing," she said, "I was up in the clouds, just sailing above the rooftops."

"What happened then?" I asked.

"Next thing," she said, "I woke up in my bed."

It was too early for her to be drinking, I thought.

I said, "Maybe it was just a dream."

She put her rake down very seriously and looked at me.

"You know, I thought of that too," she said, "but when I woke up, my arms were so tired."

I might have argued that her arms might have hurt from all the raking she'd been doing, but logic had no use here. The story was too wonderful.

Another evening, a bunch of neighbors were out on the street watching the children play. One of the mothers reported that her son, a three-year-old, said he remembered being born. Everyone laughed. The discussion turned to first memories, and most everyone had one that was dramatic and exciting. One guy recalled dancing in a graveyard when he was five. A woman remembered a hand placing a warm washcloth on her forehead. When the memories lagged, someone asked Miss Leone her first memory and she answered without hesitation.

"I opened a refrigerator door, I was just strong enough to do it, and then a tray of deviled eggs crashed down on me." When I laughed out loud, Miss Leone did too, breaking the silence that had fallen on the group when she began to speak. But I don't know if she made this up or was really remembering. That was the fun of Miss Leone.

EACH CHRISTMAS she brought me a present. She had nothing for my wife or children. It was just me. She explained that she had chosen me to get the worst Christmas present she received each year, and she knew I would enjoy them.

"This way, when I get something hopeless, I will be delighted with it, knowing it will bring you a kick," she said. She was right. Over the years, I looked forward to unwrapping Miss Leone's rejects.

These included:

A stuffed toy, but not an animal. It was a big yellow banana with a peel that you unzipped.

A pepper mill about a yard high, the kind they use at restaurants, where the waiter introduces himself by name and then bows low with the pepper mill, aiming it like a bazooka at your salad.

A coffee mug shaped like a toucan; his big yellow beak is the handle.

Socks made out of a furlike material, so that when you cross your legs, you look like you are really King Kong under your suit.

Since Miss Leone had no family that we knew of, and few friends, I wondered where these gifts came from and suspected that maybe she bought them herself. Regardless, they gave us both a great deal of pleasure, and she always asked about them with a straight face, yet a tiny smile curled at the end of her lips.

ONE NIGHT when I came home from work, I saw an ambulance in front of her house. My wife told me that Miss Leone had called for it herself.

It turned out she had cancer, and had never mentioned it to anyone, had not even seen a doctor. When she called the ambulance, the medics were shocked at the advanced state of her condition.

I visited her in the hospital, and although she was in great pain, she still spoke for a while. Her conversation had the same nonsequiturs, but they seemed more profound than ever.

At one point, she asked, "Do you have a theme song?"

"A theme song?" I asked.

"A song that followed you or that someone gave to you. Did you give your son a song when he was born?"

I hadn't, but I told her that the radio was playing in the hospital room when Harry was born, and I recalled that as he was being delivered, Shirley Bassey was singing "Goldfinger" from the James Bond movie.

"When I was born," she said, "my father said my theme song would be 'You'll Never Walk Alone.' Do you know that one?"

"Yes, that's a good one."

"It is," she said, "but that's just what I've gone and done."

And I guess she had. I had never met anyone like her.

When a priest visited her room and asked if she wanted to confess her sins, she said, "Put me down for everything but murder."

She was dead in two weeks. During my last visit she pulled me close and asked a favor of me.

"Make sure they leave my glasses on my nose when they bury me," she said.

"I will," I promised.

"If there's another place after this, I want to be sure I can see my way around. That's all I need, to be dead and to be blind too!"

"I'll take care of it, Miss Leone," I said, and I did.

You saw through all of us, Miss Leone, and helped us see ourselves. And more than that, you gave us the chance to look through your eyes and let us see like we had never seen before. Of course you should keep those glasses on.

Staying Home

THOREAU DIDN'T GET AROUND MUCH. He moved to Walden Pond for a year, and visited here and there in New England, but mostly he stayed home.

"I traveled extensively in my own room," he wrote.

I had to use the same line when I went back to work after taking a week's vacation. It was June, and my seven-year-old still had school, so we couldn't leave town. I would lose the week if I didn't take it, so on Monday morning, when Harry went off to school, and my wife left for her job, I stayed home.

It was good to read the newspaper in a leisurely way for a change, looking out the window at the bird feeder and holding a cup of coffee. But the second page of the paper held an odd story: a man who was mentally ill shot himself in the head, and not only lived, but destroyed the part of his brain that caused his illness. "The .22-caliber slug destroyed the section of the brain responsible for his disabling obsessive-compulsive behavior without causing any other brain damage." The man used to take hundreds of showers a day and washed his hands even more than that. After he shot himself he became a "straight-A student," the paper reported.

What a story! Think of the chances of his shot! It was a weird story to start off the day, but positive in its peculiar way.

I picked up some magazines I hadn't yet read, and thumbed through them. There were beautiful pictures of the Sonora desert in Arizona, a place I always wanted to visit, and I imagined the quiet.

I thought of my daughter, a sophomore at college who was spending the summer in her college town, and I wrote her a note. It said, in part:

"Earlier this morning, Harry was brushing his teeth and leaving a tricolored stripe of toothpaste from the bathroom to the kitchen. I call him the wandering toothbrusher. I'm sitting in the kitchen, mixing half decaf and half regular, like a chemist. I know this makes you miss the place and not miss it at the same time. This is how it should be, don't you think?"

I picked up a book on Casey Stengel, the great baseball manager, sent to me by a friend. I read how Mickey Mantle struck out in an important game, came back to the dugout and kicked over the water cooler. Casey looked at him and said, "It ain't the water cooler which is getting you out."

I drank more coffee, walked around the house, and made a sandwich.

Back in the bedroom, with all the books and old things spread out on the bed, I heard footsteps bounding through the house—someone was here! Then I heard a questioning "Hello?" in a high voice. It was my son, Harry, home from school. I had never been in the house since he had started to walk home alone from the bus and it shocked me to see him trudging through the dining room with his knapsack, smiling at me. His independence was welcome, but a surprise. He had snapped me out of my reverie and I was glad for that too.

He put down his backpack, unzipped it, and gave me a piece of paper.

"Happy Father's Day!" he said.

I had forgotten, too, that next Sunday was Father's Day. Harry had been born on a Father's Day, and the hospital had given me a card then, signed with his footprint.

This card was different. It was a computer printout he had written at school. It read:

MY DAD
Dad is nice and so
are mice.
"Get me I'm falling,
Bye!" And Dad caught
me.

What a great way to come back to earth. We hugged and then went to the kitchen for some cookies.

Each day I waited for him to come home.

When I got back to work, everyone asked where I went.

"I traveled a lot in my own house," I said, and the gang laughed.

It was not a lie, it was time-travel and travel in my imagination, and the path was short to the ones I loved. Somehow I had never realized it in my rush.

By staying home, I went farther than I ever had in a packed car.

About the Author

JOHN SKOYLES was born and raised in Queens, New York. A poet and professor, he is the author of *A Little Faith* and *Permanent Change*, and has taught at Sarah Lawrence College, Southern Methodist University, and Warren Wilson College. He is currently chair of the Writing, Literature and Publishing Division of Emerson College. He lives with his family in Truro, Massachusetts.